Bryn 20

SCRIBBLE

The World at Our Feet

Vol II

Edited by Steve Twelvetree

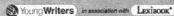 Young**Writers** in association with **LEXIBOOK**

First published in Great Britain in 2004 by
YOUNG WRITERS
Remus House,
Coltsfoot Drive,
Peterborough, PE2 9JX
Telephone (01733) 890066

SB ISBN 1 84460 322 9

Foreword

Perhaps no period in life is more fertile, more vibrant with the promise of unlimited imaginative potential that the crucial formative years preceding the onset of adolescence. This volume aims to encapsulate at least some of the flavour of these exciting, sometimes tumultuous years, presenting the best of a generally excellent sample of poetry submitted by a broad cross-section of seven to eleven-year-olds for our Scribbler! The World At Our Feet Vol II *competition in 2003.*

The following poems encompass an entertaining and diverse range of themes as the children within express their hopes for the future, visualise their wildest dreams of fame and celebrity and dream of a better world, vanquished of today's evils of war and poverty. As the children of today grow into the adults of tomorrow, we hope Scribbler! The World At Our Feet Vol II *will grow to provide a valuable poetic snapshot of the thoughts, aspirations and dreams of a generation of children as they stand on the threshold of achieving their destiny.*

Steve Twelvetree
Editor

Contents

A Little Kindness . . .

I sit and think,
Why
When I have everything before me,
A future fresh and new,
When I can be whatever I want to,
Why shouldn't others too?
If I could find a way of helping,
Be one of those who cares
And help them place their dreams before them,
Use my life to help theirs.

I sit and think,
How
Can people be so mean and selfish,
When others meet a wall,
When people live through times of hardship,
Why do they let them fall?
If I could find a way of stopping
These cruel and thoughtless hours,
Then I would do whatever was needed,
From famine to flowers.

I sit and think,
Who
Can make a difference to injured lives
And people's injured pasts,
Who can make an honest difference,
A difference that will last?
If I don't strive to make a difference
And use my future well,
If I don't try to help out others,
Then I don't know who shall.

Victoria Haseldine (11)

LEXIBOOK
Power Academy

If The World Was At My Feet!

I f the world was at my feet the boys would be neat
F lowers would be tall

T he worries would be small
H elp would be done
E verything would have just begun

W e would work together as a team
O nly think of each other as we would like to be seen
R ather be good and always have fun
L ots of arguments can be dumb
D reams will always come true

W e would all share one queen
A s a fun and friendly person that we've all seen
S uperstars would be cool

A ll mistakes would be small and
T he rubber would not be needed at all

M y home would be big!
Y ours would be massive!

F ood for lots and lots
E veryone would be happy
E verything that's listed but
T here's still more things I wouldn't miss!

Louise Wright (8)

RUNNER UP

Girl In The Corner

Do you see that girl in the corner?
Right at the back of the class?
A dreamy expression on her face,
Her eyes are a misty glass.
She dreams of her future creation,
For she has the world at her feet,
She is the next generation
And will never accept defeat,
For in her eyes and in her mind,
There is only one future to be,
She doesn't want much,
Oh she doesn't want much
And in her dreams she can see . . .
Children are laughing together,
They are huddled around a book,
Everyone's longing to read it,
Or just to take a quick look,
Reading it makes them happy,
The cover is shiny and new,
It pictures a beautiful rainbow,
With colours, red, yellow and blue,
The author was once a little girl,
Who sat at the back of the class,
Her face was wistful and dreamy,
Her eyes were a misty glass,
Do you stop and wonder,
Who this girl may be?
I'll tell you now,
Have you guessed?
This little girl is me!

Natalie White (12)

RUNNER UP

LEXIBOOK
The Power Globe

I Just Wish

In this land of wars and fighting,
People lose their faith,
I just wish,
They would stop and look,
For that unharmed world,
Inside them.

This world is theirs
And theirs to keep,
They can visit it at any time,
This place is owned by themselves,
Mine is my favourite place to go,
It's my imagination, free to roam.

My world is a place,
Greenpeace would never need to touch,
Governments and rules do not exist,
Scenery is ever changing,
No landscape to remember or to forget
And excitement is always thriving.

Visit Paris, visit New York,
Be a prince or maybe a millionaire,
As ugly as a goblin, as wonderful as Cinderella,
Live in a box, or an estate,
Just think of the possibilities,
You are the master of our own world.

Life is a harsh but beautiful thing,
Find that peaceful place inside you,
Put faith in what you find,
Just learn that you are yourself,
The world will be relaxed,
My wish is this, live your imagination.

Charlotte Aspinall (10)

RUNNER UP

LEXIBOOK
The Power Globe

Lexibook Power Globe
An educational computer to help you
travel and discover the world through a
four-voyage Discovery Challenge.
Includes music and sounds of the
world, world cultures and customs, the
environment, history, monuments,
inventions, games and foreign
languages. Children can also access
32 other educational activities and a
bonus activity 'The Mission' combining
puzzles, riddles and questions!

When I Grow Up

When I grow up,
I want to be . . .
In films and shows,
The speakers are very big.

When I grow up,
I want to be . . .
Holding a mike in my hands,
Or on the mike stand.

When I grow up,
I want to be . . .
On stage with bubbles
And lots of smoke.

When I grow up,
I want to be . . .
Getting costume,
No lipstick or make-up.

When I grow up,
I want to be . . .
On stage nervous,
Scared, no need.

Dale Ramsey (8)

When I'm An Artist

When I'm an artist
I'm going to be
The best
One ever

Would you?

When I'm an artist
I'm going to paint
The most beautiful
Pictures ever

Would you?

When I'm an artist
I'm going to show my pictures
To everyone in the world

Would you?

When I'm an artist
I'm going to draw the
Brightest pictures ever

Would you?

When I'm an artist
I'm going to colour my pictures
So excellent that I will be
The richest person ever

Would you?

Would you want to be
An artist like me?

Would you?

Callum Howell (8)

When I Grow Older

When I grow older I want to be a pilot
Flying around the world with lots of people on my plane

When I grow older I want to be a pilot
Filling with fuel to get ready to fly

When I grow older I want to be a pilot
Jetting away to faraway countries like America

When I grow older I want to be a pilot
Flying a big plane, flying over sea and flying over land.

Joshua Mobberley-Clarke (8)

If You Were The Prime Minister

If you were the Prime Minister
Would you . . .
Silence cars
So you could hear a pin drop?

I would!

If you were the Prime Minister
Would you . . .
Give your family money
So they're as rich as the Queen?

I would!

If you were the Prime Minister
Would you . . .
Build better schools
So they're as fun as the fair?

I would!

If you were the Prime Minister
Would you . . .
Make football as unpopular as paying your bills?

I would!

When I'm the Prime Minister
That's what I will do!

Rebecca Williams (8)

Top Jobs

Dog, cat, mouse or rat,
Zookeeper, vet or looking after a pet.

Car, bus, train or tram,
Or do you want to be a taxi man?

Office, packer, manager or slacker,
Or going up the stages to become an actor.

Athlete, doctor, nurse or flying a chopper,
Or being a millionaire.

Poker player or table layer,
What do you want to be?

Teacher, preacher or a web page feature,
The future is in our hands.

Sailor, writer, artist or fighter,
Finding a job may be tough,
But the job I find will be good enough!

Zophia Gillam (10)

I Want To Play For West Ham

I want to play for West Ham
Even though I'm ten
I'll be the best, I'll beat the rest
Again and again and again
I want to play for West Ham
I'll be better than Becks and Cole
I'll score the goals in every match
Yes, my name is Nicole
I want to play for West Ham
Even though I'm young
Most of all my dream is to be West Ham's number one.

Nicole Lloyd (10)

I Want To Be Famous

I want to be famous,
I want to be in books,
I want to be famous,
I want to be a cook,
I want to make people smile
And live with all the stars,
Be a famous film director
Or an astronaut on Mars,
I want to be a famous pop star
And have a number one hit,
Score a goal for England,
Hitting the ball in the net,
I want to be a golfer
And have a hole in one,
I want to be a scientist
And launch a robot to the sun,
But if I can't be famous,
I'll just have to try my best.

John Western (7)

What I Would Like To Be

I'd like to be a nurse one day
And save people's lives
People come in because they're eating too much
And especially apple pies
I'd like to work in the children's part
Because the children are very kind
I've only been in the children's bit once
When I go to see Westlife
On my way home I would see someone in the road
I would get out of my car
And shout, 'Are you alright?'
And then I would call the code
Then I would be a lifesaver
And people would cheer
I'd go home with my friends
And we'd help ourselves to a beer.

Bethan Mullins (8)

What I Would Like To Be

When I grow up I want to work on the dock
And tell people to get off
I want to bring boats in
The fish sing
When something goes wrong
I'd blow the whistle!

Ryan Beecroft (8)

What I Would Like To Be

When I grow up I would like to be a nurse
I would use
A little purse
Look after
The patients
They would
Receive eighteen invitations
I would make
Their beds
Brush their teds
They would have
Little heads.

Sophie Foston (8)

Fighting Evil

I want to fight evil in my own land,
But it's crime, I'll get myself killed.
I want to fight with a sword,
But all it is, is an elastic band!
I want to fight evil in my own bedroom,
But my mum always says . . .
'Do it in the living room!'

My mum says, 'It's not very real!'
But I ignore her, so I made her a deal!

I want to fight evil in my own back garden,
My mum always says, 'Make your own den!'
But as you know, I don't listen to her,
All I hear is blah blah blah!

Rachel Bott (9)

Having Super Powers

Super strong,
Righting the wrong,
Having super powers,
Helping other people for hours and hours,
Beating up the bad,
Now no one is sad,
I have saved the world once again,
Now bad guys feel the pain,
I fly off to my hiding place,
I fly at a fast speed,
Now I've done my good deed,
Now to have a big, big feed,
Hurry up, it's nearly noon,
Better start fighting soon,
All the evil go to jail,
I'm going to a shelter, it's starting to hail,
All my powers are really good,
I do everything that I should.

Oliver Johnson (8)

I'd Love To Drive A Car

I'd love to drive a car,
I'd drive it very far,
I'd drive it very fast
And see things flashing past.

I'd drive it to the moon,
I'd drive it to a lagoon,
I'd drive it to a park,
But never leave a mark.

I'd drive it on a track
And go past point Mach,
I'd drive it up to Heaven,
I'd drive it twice times seven.

Christopher Webster (9)

Save The World

Save the planet, please
We want to keep our trees
Millions of trees are cut down
If you can, save the trees

Every hour of every day
Trees are getting cut down
Our environment is getting worse
Instead, make our environment better

So make it better if you can
Don't chuck rubbish on the floor
Keep it tidy
Put your rubbish in bins, please!

Charlotte Fryer (8)

Fighting Evil

F ighting crime to stop evil
I n the land of superheroes
'G ive me all your money,' said the robber
H it, bang, smash, crash!
T o stop the world from evil
I nto the police car, robber
N ow the town is being destroyed
G et him or her

E eek goes the monster
V room, all the cars are going by themselves
I f we can make a plan, we can destroy him or her
L et's save the day.

Jack James (8)

When I'm Older

When I'm older I'm going to live in Africa
Just think of the things you see in Africa
I mean you could live with the gorillas in Africa
You could see the exciting dances and styles in Africa
You could walk in the big forests in Africa
You could see the leopards and lions in Africa
You could swim with the whales in Africa
Just think what you could see in Africa.

Caitlin Meechan (11)

I Look Down

I look down to my dream job as a physiotherapist,
I look down . . . down past the mist.

I look down to my dream cosy cottage,
With family and all.

I will visit places here and there
And maybe . . . just maybe everywhere.

I look down as I fly with my dreams,
I look down as I fly with my dreams.

I don't want a lot in life, just my dreams,
If I didn't, life would just seem . . .

Dull and boring.

Samantha MacDonald (10)

Hopes And Dreams

Hopes and dreams are important in our life,
Hoping to be a doctor or a vet,
Dreaming of fresh flowers in the spring,
But life is sometimes not fair,
Your hopes and dreams could disappear,
But you'll always know you can still make it.

Ami McKnight (11)

My Dreams

Money is what I want
Yellow is my worst colour
Dad brings me a limousine
Red is my favourite colour
Everywhere I go I demand ice cream
All the time Newcastle United beat Celtic
Maths is my favourite subject
Suzuki Escudo sports car is what I want to drive.

James Mowbray (11)

Me And My Dreams

When I am older . . .
I will visit the world
And meet the actors
And drive in their limousine
And become famous
And everyone will know me
When I am out and about
And they are coming up for my autograph
And telling their pals and classmates about me
Maybe not but it will be fun
But a bit of a headache, everyone screaming at me
So maybe something easy, like a cleaner
Yes, that's what I will be.

Stephanie Kirkwood (11)

My Dreams

M y dreams are full of hopes
Y ellow is a colour

D ecember is my favourite month
R ichard is my name, football is my game
E leven is my age
A lways dream of playing for Rangers
M arching through the Scottish table
S aucy skills, here I come.

Richard Johnstone

My Dream House

My dream house would be in the countryside
And it would be huge
It would have 500 rooms and 100 of them would be en-suite
It would have 50 swimming pools
And some gyms and saunas
It would have a big garden with a pool outside too
It would probably have a couple of chocolate pools too
It would have a golf course and a cinema inside as well.

Christopher Carr (11)

The Poem Of The Future

When I grow up I would like to be an explorer
I would go into the wild and take photos of deer and foxes
Owls at night and live in the wild
Because the wild is full of fresh air from the trees
Because it is so sweet in the wild
There are birds, deer and foxes in the wild.

Lee Barrie (10)

When I'm Eighteen

When I'm older . . .
My dream is to
Work in a clothes shop
If anyone complains I'll be very annoyed

When I'm older . . .
My dream is to
Work in a clothes shop
I'll fold clothes and listen to music

When I'm older . . .
My dream is to
Work in a clothes shop
If everyone is queuing up I'll work much quicker

When I'm older . . .
My dream is to
Work in a clothes shop
I'll stand at the till with the noise in my head
And probably pretend I'm still in bed.

Sarah White (8)

When I Am Older

When I am older I will be a famous author
With the coolest illustrator
You have ever seen
And my books will all be published

When I am older I will be so determined
To make some good books
Both happy and sad, good and bad
And my books will all be published

When I am older children will love me and my books
And I'd win lots of prizes
For all of them, yes
So my books will all be published.

Heather Robinson (8)

Life

Life sometimes can be a real pain
Even though I love it all the same
I take each day as it comes
Because there's loads of things I hope to become
I don't frown and I don't fret
Maybe I'll be a vet
That's not exactly what I want to do
But who can tell? Not I nor you
Art's a subject that I like
Or perhaps I'll become famous by riding my bike!

Hannah Blakey (10)

My Dreams

M y dreams are all about football
Y oung is my rival's name who plays for Real Madrid

D ad shows me his skills in football
R angers is my club's name
E ach game we play ends in a draw
A ll the time I practise, I can score 3 goals at the most
M an, I hate it when I get yellow cards
S omeday Rangers will beat Real Madrid.

Gary O'Toole (10)

My Dreams

A music teacher I want to be,
I'll follow my dreams and you will see,
My singing I get told is very good,
The choir has done as much as they could.

My piano lessons I really enjoy,
I can play lots of rhythms and songs,
My teacher has really helped me,
I'd like to say thanks a lot.

Last of my hobbies, dancing is brilliant,
In freestyle exams 97 percent I got,
Bronze and silver I already have,
Gold I'm working towards.

When I'm not doing any of this,
My nights off I can't resist.

Megan Wilkie (10)

The World At My Feet

Me when I'm older?
That's easy for me
I want to go to college
Then university
Yes that's right for me!

I want to move to America
And work as a lawyer
I want to walk across the Great Wall of China
I will wait there until the stars appear
Yes, that's right for me!

Or I can be a famous movie star
I can just imagine me coming out of a stretch limousine
Everyone asking for my autograph!
Yes, that's right

No, I have changed my mind
I want to be me
I care about my career
I need to accept what my life is
Yes, that's right!

Kirstie Duncan (11)

The Hollywood Dream

On your way to the studio
Where you just came out of a limousine
People looking at you with banners in the air
You look ahead and then you see lots of paving slabs
The glittering names with stars above them
Have a guess who will be next?
It might take quite a few
You never know that it might even be you!

Josh Jameson (11)

My Hopes And Dreams

I have a dream that when I grow up
I would like to be very rich
Someone like a footballer on the football pitch
When I'm older, I hope my hopes and dreams come true
I hope I have a big house and a very nice car too
I want to travel around the world, maybe visit Japan
I know I will be very special, better than any man
I have many hopes and dreams
I wish they will become true, maybe they will someday
If it does, it will feel very new
I'd like to be many people when I grow up
Like a racer or a footballer playing in the muck.

Fionn Macauley (11)

My Dreams

When I dream, I dream about
What I will do when I'm older
I imagine I will own a restaurant
With pink walls and a ceiling
And candles lining the room
Glowing in the darkness

When I dream, I dream about
The world being a better place
If I could I would
Stop all of the wars and planet Earth
I would stop people's hunger
In unfortunate places

When I dream, I dream about
Having a trip to Australia
To see the koalas
And meet the kangaroos
I'd like to go on a safari
And travel round the bush

I would be very happy
If all these drams come true
But I guess you can't have
Everything in life
That's the truth.

Ellen Constable (11)

Looking Forward

When I am older
I hope I will be
A primary school teacher
That would please me

In the classroom
With the children
Marking work
By the million

When I have time
If I have any
I'll travel the world
And countries plenty

I could scuba dive
At the Barrier Reef
I hope I don't meet a shark
And don't see its teeth!

I could go to New York
For Christmas shopping
Go to the snack bar
And hear the popcorn popping

I could go back to Sarasota
And jump in the pool
And swim for ages
Until I'm nice and cool

But my ultimate dream
Is to go to the World Cup
And see stars from lots of places
Lifting the most important trophy
With tears running down their faces.

Naomi Forbes (11)

Dreams

Last night I dreamt I was a vet,
My friend dreamt she was a superstar, I bet,
I dreamt I was a vet the night before,
It's beginning to get a bit of a bore.
Oh I wish I was older,
I might then be bolder.
I love dogs and cats,
But I'm scared of rats.
I have no favourite animal
Because all mammals are the best.
All the rest are okay I guess,
Oh, how I'd love to be a vet.

Hollie Aitken (10)

That'll Be A Sight To See!

Next year I hope to get a pony
Yes, what is a pony without me?
I want to join NASA and go into space
Yes I want to see the stars, the planets
And Mother Earth in all her beauty
That'll be a sight to see!
I want to go to China and see the Great Wall
And stand on the tallest mountain
Or the smallest, I don't care
All I want is world peace
Yes! World peace
That would be nice to see, countries getting along
That'll be a sight to see!
The rich helping the poor
Giving them food, shelter and warmth
People caring for nature and all the animals
That'll be a sight to see!
All I want is peace and harmony
In the world, man and animal side by side
Looking after the biggest mammal
To the smallest insect
That'll be a sight to see!

Sareena Hashmat (11)

India And Tigers

My hopes, my dreams are too soon going to be over
You know why?
Because a beautiful and big cat will be extinct when I'm older
So my dream of India and tigers would be gone forever
Many species are already dead, never to be brought back
Now my ambition of working in buffer forests are gone, no chance, never
Maybe in a few years' time, tigers will be gone
Tigers' coats are beautiful, the black against the orange
But it looks so much better on the original owner
Then people will think about what they've done.

Sarah Bryson (11)

My Cat

My cat, my cat it wears a big hat
It travels night and day even though
It might get scared away

My cat is the best even though
It's got a woolly vest
He has a pin for a tooth
And he can jump to a roof

Now my cat is dead
I wish I had a dog instead.

Amy Darlow (7)

The Future

In the future I want to be a football player
Or I could be the mayor
But I would prefer to be a football player.

Or I could be a fantastic prancer
Or a brilliant disco dancer.

So I was toddling on my way home
But I forgot I could be a fantastic hairdresser
And use a comb and hair foam.

Or I could be a film star or a pop star and play on my guitar
But I could be a shopkeeper and sell soya
Or I could be a lawyer, I could be rich.

But what about playing on the football pitch?
Oh, I don't know what to do
But if I carry on like this I'll be scrubbing the loo
I can't figure out what to do.

I could be a book writer
Or I could be a boxing fighter
I could be a money maker
But I'm a job faker.

I could be a fireman
Or I could reinvent the cancan
No, no, no, I don't know what to do.

I could be in the army and fight in war
But I would die so heavily poor
But I would prefer a football player
That will be my future.

Well, the future!

Jack Hughes (8)

My Wish

When I'm older . . .
I'd like to be a famous athlete
Winning every race
I'd stride along, keeping a very steady pace
I'd beat Paula Radcliffe
I'd wave as I pass
Everyone would think of me as the number one class
I'd live in a great almighty house
I'd practise running every day
I'd go to every single restaurant and never have to pay
I'd win for England
I'd zoom past the finish line
I'd party all night with delicious food and wine.

Ella Genders (9)

A Dream!

My dream is to become a superstar,
Out there singing amongst the audience,
But I'll never be one

My dream is to be an actor
Playing Jemima and flying in a
Fabulous car.

My dream is to be an excellent artist
Drawing pandas for children
And creating new art programmes
Actually, I might become one when I'm older,
Just maybe!

Beatrice Grabowska (9)

When I Grow Up

When I grow up I might be the next biggest pop star!
Go onto Pop Idol and win . . .
I don't know what I'll do with the money!
My old clothes will go in the bin.
I'll have a massive bedroom
With a big double bed.
I'll have my own fantastic concerts,
There will be lights, pink, blue and red,
I'll wear the most fashionable clothes,
Everyone will copy my style,
I'll have sack loads of fan mail,
All stacked up in a pile.
When I'm not so famous
And everything has rusted,
Maybe I'll start dating
Cute old Charlie from Busted!

Jossie Leyburn (9)

When I'm Older

When I'm older, I want to . . .
Be an artist who makes things
To help disabled people do art.
Help poor children in Africa.
See the Grand Canyon.
Get a dog.
Live a happy life.
Drive a white open-top car.
Live in Sark.
Meet Michael Morpurgo.
Be a nanny in America.
Meet Busted.
Travel the world.

But most of all be in the Olympics!

Isabel Abbs (9)

Thoughts

Now is the right time
To leave your childhood
You've got your whole life to climb

Places you've got to go
Holidays to have
Lots of things you'd never know

The world is at your feet
You can complete your dream
Even if you can't go far
Like stars, you'll gleam

Go where your feet take you
Pick your path
Time is at the helm
So keep calm

I'd like to be a swimmer
To swim the Channel too
And to have a medal presented
By . . . by who?

I'd like to swim faster than a crocodile, alligator, shark
And pass my driving test
And not get stuck on how to park

Swimming is a dream
A dream of you and I
To think it can be done
My, oh my.

Katie Hoskin (9)

My Dream

My dream is to go around the world,
To see things that no one's seen before.
Soaring on a rocket, zooming through space with aliens.
Knowing every living thing on Earth as a friend.
Going to Hollywood to be a major star.
Being a millionaire and presenting many programmes.
Going and helping every poor person
And giving them accommodation,
Just like handing out sweets to friends.

This is my dream, what's yours?

Eleanor Shotton (9)

The Dream

What is your dream to be when you're older?
I expect lots of you want to become
Something or be a pop star?

My dream is to be a swimmer
And a person that does high jump
And takes part in all the events for high jump and swimming
I also want to be a pop star
But I don't think I'll ever become one.

Rachael Durling (9)

My Dream

I'd love to be in the Olympics
Running the 800 metres
Winning the gold medal
Standing on the stands
With flowers in my hands
Tears in my eyes

I'd love to be a pop star
Singing the night away
Going to gigs
Having thousands of fans
Being in competitions

I'd love to be in the Olympics
Swimming 200 metres backstroke
That's all that I'd like
Apart from having two children
Marrying Charlie from Busted
That's my dream

I hope it will come true.

Olivia Rendall (9)

My Dreams

One of my dreams is to be a pop star
I would spike up and dye my hair
Purple and green and look all scary and mean
I would go to every concert
Sing and dance
But all I need now
Is my own little head to think come on be a pop star
But that is not what it wants
That is one of my dreams.

Another one of my dreams
Would be to become a famous cook
Washing fruit and cutting vegetables
Pouring drinks and serving meals
My favourite meal would be roast lamb
Potatoes and mint sauce
But not forgetting the gravy!
That is another one of my dreams.

My last but not least
Is to be a world football player
Playing for England
Scoring goals and dribbling up
And passing to David Beckham
And also getting cheered by my fans
That is another one of my dreams.

These are my dreams
And I hope they come true
I hope you like them from me to you.

Charlotte Hollingsworth (10)

My Wishes

I want to be a teacher
Not a shouty one, mind
Nice and kind
My pupils will learn
Not to be audacious
I want to be a doctor
Caring for people
I would like to be a writer
And write a brief story
I would like to be lots of things
And just be happy!

Amber Small (9)

My Dreams

My dream is to be a netball superstar,
To shoot,
To defend,
To attack,
To have important interviews
And to be well-known around the world.

My second dream that I have every night,
Is to drive around in a limo,
Present awards to pop stars and movie stars
And to fly in a private jet to the most beautiful places.

I dream on and find I want to become a detective,
To find evidence that nobody else can find,
To solve cases,
To stop people from getting hurt,
I'd be in the newspaper every day,
The best detective in Kent
And then I dream on I want to become . . .

Lucy Spence (10)

My Dreams

I want to be famous
I could go behind the scenes
I could do what I like
I could fulfil all my dreams

I want to be a pop star
I could sing Avril's songs
I could do all the latest dance moves
I could have my own throngs

I want to be a model
I could walk up and down the catwalk
I could put on loads of make-up
And talk and talk and talk

But I think I'll become a millionaire!
With lots and lots of money
Then simply, my life would be as sweet as honey
But I don't like honey, I like chocolate
But otherwise it would sound funny.

Olivia Harris (9)

My Dreams

In my life I want to have a hamster that is as white as snow
Or how about a millionaire with hundreds and thousands of pounds
I dream of having a holiday in South Africa but I do not know yet
I could be a model and wear all the latest clothes
But I am not sure about that yet
And with all that money I could buy a mansion
But I think I will just stick with having a holiday in South Africa.

Tabitha Janney (9)

My Dreams

My dream is to be an actress
Or a part-time vet
I could be anything
I just don't know yet

I could be in the opera
But I don't fancy that
I could be in showbiz
At the drop of a hat!

I dream of being a millionaire
With a sauna and swimming pool
Or a glamorous model
Wearing the latest clothes and looking really cool!

But if I can't be any of those
I'll just stick to being
Me!

Rebecca Wilson (9)

I Was

I was born a small little thing
I was at nursery, playing and screaming with my friends
I was at primary school, having lots of fun
I was at senior school, growing up and working hard
I was at university, studying hard
I was at work, having a good time
But I am waiting for that to come!

Lucy Tomkins (10)

My Dreams And Ambitions

Sometimes I dream of being a fairy,
Flying up and down,
Around with no sound,
But no, I'll be too tiny.

Other times I dream of being a jockey,
Winning money, cups and shields,
It will be fun with my horse called Peter Pan,
But no, I might fall off and break my arm.

Most of the time I dream of being a vet,
For horses, dogs and rabbits,
It will be great working with animals,
But no, I'll have to operate and I hate gory sights.

I think I'll become a housewife,
I could see my husband every day,
My children too!
Yes! I think I've found my ambition,
I'm going to be a housewife.

Nicola Boulter (9)

I Want To Be . . .

I think . . .
I want to be an RSPCA vet!
Then I could have my own little pet!
No . . .
I want to be a famous chef!
No . . .
I want to be a footie ref!
No . . .
I want to be a superhero!
To infinity and beyond!
But the chances of that is barely zero!
I really don't know what to choose
I haven't got any clues
All this thinking is hurting my head
What I want to do now is go to bed.

Katharine Garratt (10)

I Could Become . . .

When I'm bored in class,
Instead of playing with my rubber,
I think of what I could be . . .
I could be the next Avril,
I could be famous,
I could hire a butler to drive me around in a limo,
I would wear the coolest clothes,
I would sing at the coolest concerts.

But I'll never be able to do that,
But I could become an . . .
Astronaut,
A famous scientist,
A doctor,
A vet or even
A famous artist.

But I could never become one of those,
So I think I'll stick to becoming Queen!

Lydia Clark (10)

I Wish

Have you ever thought you were the Queen?
Have you ever thought you were a team?

That's what I want to be.

Have you ever thought of swimming easily?
Have you ever thought of flying quickly?

That is what I want to do.

Have you ever thought you were the greatest?
Have you ever thought you're never the latest?

That's what I want to be.

Have you ever thought of jumping from aeroplanes?
Have you ever thought of owning great big lanes?

That is want I want to do.

Have you ever thought you were a superstar?
Have you ever thought of travelling very far?

That is what I want to do.

That is what I wish.

Kerry Alton (9)

My Special Poem

If I was a pop star I would always think of a new song for my latest album.
If I was a movie star I would play the really mad part in a film.
If I was a shopkeeper I would be putting things on the shelf all day
And playing with the till.
If I was a frog I would be swimming all day and sunbathing.
These are all I dream of, I will always want to do them every day
And every night until I get too old.

Annabel Featherstone (9)

Poor Children

In the heat of the day
When there's nowhere to play
The poor African children have nothing to drink
All they do is sit around and think
They live on the street
With nothing on their feet
All their tummies are empty
When all around the world there is plenty
All they can do is dream about days in the heat
In a field full of wheat.

Amy Pitt (7)

Weekly Dreams

Monday I dreamt about flying in the air
Drifting along with the wind in my hair.

Tuesday was scary, I dreamt about falling
Then I woke with a scream and a shout.

Wednesday I dreamt about being an angel in the sky
I had a flying horse, it flew really high.

Thursday I dreamt about bouncing above the trees
Listening to the tunes of the birds and bees.

Friday I dreamt about sitting near a hot fire
Drinking warm milk, I was very, very tired.

Jade Rowlands (11)

When I Am Older

When I am older
I'll help people in need
And all the young children
I will help feed

All the old people
Who need shelter and heat
I'll give them homes
And clothes they can keep

If all the wars
And troubles come to an end
People would be able to
Live life as friends.

Jessica Swift (10)

The Future

I will be on Pop Idol
And become a famous star.
I will be in an orchestra
And I'll play on my guitar!

I will marry my one true love
And we will love each other forever.
We'll have lots and lots of children
And we'll all help the world together.

If I could, I'd stop the wars
And not let people die.
I'd know just how to help them
By looking them in the eye.

I would cure them as fast as I could
And give them money, food and a home.
If they needed anything,
They could call me on the phone.

I'd ask all the villains in the world,
Why do they rob for what they need?
I'll help them turn over a new leaf
And start from a new seed.

I would work with animals,
Like a vet in a zoo,
But if I couldn't keep an animal alive,
Then I'd have to start something new.

So when I look into the future,
My life will be so great
And by stopping all the badness
There will be no hate.

Ellen Williams (10)

I Wish

I want to be an astronaut
I wish I could go up in space
The wind would be blowing in my face
I'd fly around Mars and
Touch all the stars

I want to be a vet
I wish I could be a vet
I would look after every pet
From cats to bats
From bears to hares
From snails to whales

I want to be a clown
I wish I could be a clown
I'd never wear a frown
I'd throw around pies
So they'd touch the skies
I'd be a clown forever
And I'd never cry!

Hayley Smith & Hannah Donnelly (9)

I Wish To Fly To Space

I wish to fly up to space
With the wind in my face

I wish to fly among the stars
And hope to land on planet Mars

I wish to fly right up high
And finally touch the sky

I wish to fly up to space
With the wind in my face.

Amber Schroeder (9)

All About School

School is good
And school is generous
School is happy
School is fun
And you can have
A good time there
You can be happy there
School is a good place.

Lauren Gillson (7)

What I Want To Be

I want to be a crocodile
And swim down the rushing Nile
Trick food with my friendly smile
Yes - I want to be a crocodile
But Mum said I can't
And Dad said I shan't

I want to be a little mouse
And I can scurry around the house
Eat lots of woodlouse
Yes - I want to be a little mouse
But Dad said I shan't
And Mum said I can't

I want to be a butterfly
And fly high into the sky
Up and up really high
Yes - I want to be a butterfly
But Dad said I can't
And Mum said I shan't

I want to be a kangaroo
And crush the entire zoo
That's what I want to do
Yes - I want to be a kangaroo
But Mum said I shan't
And Dad said I can't

I can't be a wombat
I can't be a pussy cat
I can't be a dotty dog
I can't be a smelly hog
I can't be a bumblebee
I know! I'll be a tree.

Katie Wright (10)

My Dream

My dream is to help the poor
You might think the journey will make me sore
Dream about the world around us
Remind yourself about the Indian bus
Eager to find food they are
And they might live in a distance quite far
My dream is to stay here and pay for charity.

Zoe Ellis (8)

In Seven Years' Time . . .

In seven years' time,
I'll be the best,
Better than the rest
At doing my famous job.

In seven years' time,
My ideas will be the best,
With my clothes, dripping gold
From all the money I've earned.

In seven years' time,
All the colours will be cool,
You will all want to buy my designs,
That I will have spent hours on.

In seven years' time,
When I'm walking down the street,
Everyone will be wearing my clothes
And will be calling my name.

In seven years' time,
My workers will be up all night,
Stitching and sewing as quiet as mice,
Do you know what I want to be?

Martha Somerfield (8)

I'm A Football Star

My dream is stardom on the football pitch
My face is in all the papers and on the big screen
The crowd are all cheering my name
My team is at the top of the league

But it's not as easy as it seems
There's all the training each week
It's really exceedingly hard
It's quite relieving to be home at last

I hate it when I'm not picked for the team
It's ever so boring sitting on the subs bench
Just itching to get on the pitch
I can't wait for it

When injury strikes me
I get really annoyed
Just watching from home
I want to be on the pitch

When it's a big game
I'm always hoping to be picked
When I do I always play my best
The score is 5-1
Come on England!

Thomas Dhanji (10)

Playing To Win

I'm sitting in my bedroom
I am really bored
I close my eyes
I wish I was at Wimbledon
Not in Ford

I play tennis every Tuesday
Even every Wednesday
When I grow up I'd like to play in Wimbledon
I shall practise every day
I can imagine me playing against Serena and Venus

On big loudspeakers the man says
'Karina and Serena are just about to play'

I sit there in my bedroom
I hear crowds applauding
I feel so important
I feel like a king

I open my eyes suddenly
Someone's just come through the door
I sigh. I know it's just a thought
I won't tell you anymore . . .

Karina Roche (10)

The Championship

As I'm crouching down to start
I'm thinking I've got to be as fast as a dart
As I hear the sound of the gunshot
I feel my muscles tense
I'm thinking there's no time to think
The fog in my mind is dense

As I'm coming down to the finish
I'm thinking who is first
And if I'm not
I know I'm surely cursed
I see something appear on screen
It seems to be my face
Even though I've won the gold medal
I've also won the race.

Danielle Parkes (10)

The Horse Of Dreams

As I look at my dream horse
Black as a storm cloud
His mane and tail flying in the wind
He whinnies, he looks, he gallops towards me
'The Black' I shall call him

Making my horse shine
His coat gleams in the sun
His hooves clean as a whistle
His mane and tail no longer tangly
Satisfied. It's time to ride

I jump on his back
No stirrups, saddle or reins
Bareback we'll call this
I wrap my arms around his neck
Now we gallop through the long grass

We come to a gushing river
I need to trust my horse
I urge him on, he plunges in
The water splashing at his strong legs
He wades on up to the bank

Back from the ride two months later
Now it comes to a difficult time
It's spring and a mare trots by
He whinnies, he neighs, he tries to greet her
But no, I would not give him his head
We ride on by.

Naomi Clarke (10)

The Rainforest

A tiger prowls, orange and black
A lion roars, he sees a zebra, he must attack
The monkey swings from tree to tree
An elephant bellows. He's so big he could trample me

A snake slithers through the grass
Birds overhead, so many colours, make noises when they pass
Suddenly the rain pours down
The peacock runs for shelter to protect his feathered gown

I look at all the trees around
All the animals have shelter. Some see me and off they bound
Now I'm heading back to the lodge
I am thankful tomorrow I will know which animals to dodge!

Hattie Le Gresley (10)

Gallop Away!

We're galloping through the mist
Jumping over the grassy hedges
Sloshing in the murky water
The wind is slapping my face
Deafening in my ears
We're covered in mud
I hear the pattering of hooves
Growing louder and faster
We have got to win this race

We're so near to the end
I can see the finish line
But there's still someone in front
I urge Black Thunder faster
We're in line with the other horse
There's just one more jump
The other horse stumbles over it
It falls down and doesn't recover . . .
We have crossed the finish line at last

I punch my fist in the air
I feel Black Thunder breathing fast
I'm feeling so happy
I let out a sigh of relief
I ride Black Thunder back to the horse box
And drive back home to get some rest
But Black Thunder is not tired, he wants a quick ride
So I climb on his back so we can savour the moment
I'll never ever forget that wonderful day.

Harriet McClure (10)

Go Wild!

I want to go on safari, to see it in the wild
The predator, the prey, the fearsome and the mild
The lion with his appetite, the tiger with his roar
Hyenas laughing, feasting, then going out for more

The tall giraffe with his neck so long
And all the birds singing their song
I see an elephant with his great long trunk
His feet hit the ground with a fearful clunk

A parrot flies in the sky
His colourful feathers seen going by
I see a camel wander by
With his hump sitting so high

The zebra with his black and white stripes
I see so many different types
This is why I cannot wait
For my first safari date.

Sarah Lunt (10)

Hit It!

I'm in, we're 15 runs down
The bowler bowls, everyone shouts
'Hit it!'
I do, the umpire signals a 4
Same thing again
I hit it as hard as I can
I shout 'Yes!'
We run and run
We've got 3 more

Jake's up now
I say 'Hit it'
But he doesn't and it's LBW
Now he's out

Now it's Pete
He hits it and we run
And run
It's a 4, no 5, no, no, no stay or you'll be out . . .
Too late

It's 74 runs to 70
I save 4 more, that's all

We're fielding now
I say 'Howzat' seven times
The umpire says the game has finished
We've won
77 runs to 74

Tom Malam (10)

When I Grow Up

When I grow up I want to be
A spaceman to fly to the stars above.
To meet the Martians on planet Mars
And drive around in their funny little cars.
It would be nice to have a Martian friend,
To drive you to different places
And then have Martian car races.
I would come 1st or 2nd place,
Then I would jump back into my spaceship
And say bye to my friends.

When I grow up I want to be
A teacher to tell off all the naughty children
And teach all the good ones,
That's what I want to see,
I want to go in the playground
And see all the happy children playing around,
Helping children learn is my job,
Education is important,
And while I'm teaching I'll have a Hobnob,
Help me decide, I really can't choose,
What job shall I have?

Hazel Pettitt (9)

George Wallace We Want You!

In Hockley there was a big boy
Whose mum he used to annoy
By kicking the ball right up the wall
As football he did so enjoy!

His dream was to play for Man U
And one day his dream did come true!
In the letter it said
'Here's 5 million to wear red!
George Wallace we want you!'

George Wallace (9)

A Dream

My wish is to stop all wars
And stop pollution too,
Everyone would know my name
And all the animals too.

I wish I had the power
To swim like fishes do,
Then I could swim with dolphins
And sharks and whales too.

Every time a person walks by,
They would whisper to their friends,
There's the person who travelled
To where the known world ends.

Andrew Labdon (10)

My Ferrari F50 Spider

My dream would be
To drive in a Ferrari F50 Spider
All around the world
My car is red and silver
Max speed is 202mph
I bought it when it was brand new
I'm very proud of my Ferrari F50 Spider
I think you would be too.

Tom Reed (9)

My Dream

My dream would be . . .
To swim with a dolphin,
Sleek and happy as can be,
I might have a special power,
Being able to breathe
Under the sea.

Swimming around,
Looking, staring,
Suddenly I see them
Looking back at me,
Big eyes staring,
In the sea.

I ride around,
Holding on tight,
A bottlenose dolphin
Jumping high and far,
Soon we see
A rusty old bar.

All too soon,
It is time to surface,
To leave my companions
In the water alone,
I think of them,
In the sea, alone, alone.

Sarah-Jane Harris (10)

Saints, I Love You

Pitch! Pitch!
I want to put the ball on the ground
Kick it to me!
Beep
It's time for break
Yes, yes, I've got the ball!
I'm near the goal
I've passed to my team
He scores! The goalie is ashamed
He let his team down
Yes, yes, I love you Saints
I've tackled them, I've scored
10 goals with my team
Saints, I love you, I do
Yes, we've won the cup!
It even has my name on!
Alright, I'll have to go
Yes, I love you
Saints!

Ashley Chandler (8)

My Dream

M y dream would be to swim with tonnes of fish
Y achts, yachts through the sea

D ream, dream with fish
R ound and round they go
E ating fish is delicious
A ll kinds of fish are kind and friendly
M arlin, Marlin come here!

Georgina Ford (8)

The World At Your Feet

My only wish is
That I had loads of horses
And my sister had loads
Of dolphins.

Laura Whitlam (9)

Appearing On Pop Idol

P ractise every day
O rganise your songs
P romise to be sensible

I dol people
D o you want to win?
O h no, I think I've lost!
L ittle time to lose . . .

Maria Clawley (8)

My Dream

My dream is to play football,
Score a goal with the Cup Final ball,
I'll play for Chelsea,
I hit a ball on the volley up into a tree.

Penalty! I step up to whack it,
Then I smack it,
The goalie said,
'Oh, it's a goal!'

Danny Baker (9)

Jobs

When I grow up,
I want to have a job,
Like maybe a chef
And then I'd stuff my gob!

How about a milkman
Or an astronaut?
Maybe a belly dancer,
That is what I thought.

There's loads of jobs to choose from,
But please, please, please help me,
Because there is a problem,
I don't know what to be!

Zoe Pettitt (9)

What Will I Be?

Looking in the mirror
Deciding what to be,
So much is going on,
It's distracting me.

Snipping, clipping,
Chatting, laughing,
Water splashing,
Hairdryer blowing,
Radio booming.

Red hair, pink hair,
Long hair, short hair,
Curly hair, straight hair,
Brushed hair, cut hair,
Different styled hair.

A hairdresser!
That's what I'll be.

Rachel Carter (7)

I Want To Be A Policewoman!

I want to be a policewoman
Small, smart and round
To catch robbers day and night
And pin them to the ground

I want to go undercover
To be the best around
To put naughty people behind bars
So they're not around

It must be a blast
Catching thieves all around
Driving in my new police car
All around the town.

Shannon Ross (10)

A Schoolgirl Dream

In twenty years I want to be a teacher
I'll teach small children to measure a metre
In my class I want a boy called Peter
I'll teach them all about a litre
In my class there is no cheater
But I'm just a schoolgirl who wants to be a brilliant teacher.

Amy Alice Owens (10)

The World At Our Feet

I'd love to be a marine biologist
And study the seven seas
Find my very own fish
And name it after me!
I'd love to scuba-dive
When the sun is setting
Swim with the dolphins and Mediterranean fish
I'd love to find tons of oysters
Make bracelets from many coloured pearls
I'd love to feel the glorious skin of a string ray again
I'd love to see the brightly coloured starfish
Clinging to the coral
I'd love to see the little eels
Pop out of mysterious holes
I'd love to be a marine biologist
The world would truly be
Within my very reach.

Rebecca Ballard (10)

The World At Our Feet

I wish I was a superhero
I could fly into space
And I could rescue the world
From nuclear waste
I could have saved the Twin Towers
With my super powers
I could live on stars
And visit Mars
Once in a while

I could fly all day
And save people form sharks
In Australian bays
I would be really rich
And watch people play
On a football pitch
I would ride in a Ferrari
And fly in the sky
I would be so free
I wish I was a superhero.

Jacinta Yap (10)

The World At Our Feet

Be a superhero
Be as rich as can be
Be as rich as a king
Or as rich as a queen
Be as poor as a beggar man
In a tiny little dump
Be as big as a tree
Be whatever you want

But what I'd love to do
Is to swim with dolphins
In the Mediterranean Sea
I'd love to do tricks with them
Perform with them
Feed them, help them
I would love to be free
Material wishes are of little use
Freedom is my goal.

Sarah Nawell (10)

The World At My Feet

If I had one wish
What would it be?
To fly with the birds
Or swim with the fish in the sea?
If I had only one wish
What would I choose?
To go to competitions
And never to lose?

But my one wish is
None of those things
Not to wear bracelets
And diamond rings
My one wish may not
Be special to you
But for me, I really
Hope it will come true

To dance at London's
Royal Opera House
If I had this wish
I would never grouse
To dance by rivers
To dance by a stream
As long as I dance
I can fulfil any dream.

Emma Norman (10)

The World At My Feet

I would like to . . .
Whoosh up into the air
And then see the people near my house
Look up and stare
And I would be able to see
The world without a care

I would be able to see . . .
All of the florescent ferns
Dancing in the breeze
And all of the people that are walking
Down the street and also hear them talking

I want to soar like a bird
And do barrel rolls, then go upside down
As well as soaring through
The bright blue sky
Then I see the stars come out, gleaming white
And then I would find it such a sight
I'd hover and wait, then stay all night.

Hannah Evans (10)

The World At Our Feet

I'd love to be a jockey
Winning gymkhanas all around
Grooming, plaiting and making my horse look grand
Being showered in cups and rosettes
I'd have a room just for them
And when I opened the door
They'd all fall out

I'd have a horse called Chester
The best horse around
Famous for his obedience
I'd groom him and plait him every day
And if anyone insulted him
They'd get what they deserved!

He'd always win races
People would become millionaires
Because at the 'bookies'
They'd know which one to vote for

But that would only happen
If we had the world at our feet.

Amelia Kidwell (10)

World At Our Feet

Freedom, that is what we need,
No more war,
Prisoners must have done something wrong to get in prison.
Something, but why, why did they do it?
If I were in charge, I would change this for world peace.

My wish is that children in Africa and places
With children who are starving hungry,
So I could make a wish to help them,
In whatever way I can,
This is my wish from me to you.

If I were in charge,
I would make no more pollution,
So that more animals would get well,
From whatever illness they could get or have,
This I hope will get better,
This is my wish.

Ace Abraham-Jones (10)

Not Going Back To School

The summer holidays are finished
But I'm not going back to school
I'm going travelling to
Austria, Australia, France, Spain, Egypt, Africa and Mexico too.

Even though school has started,
I don't care, I'm going
Sunbathing, diving, snorkelling, swimming
Maybe sailing,
I don't know, all I know is
I'm not going back to school.

The teachers may shout,
'Oh no you can't,
You have to stay in school!'
So I'll answer back,
'I'm going travelling, not back to school,
You can shout all you like
But I'm never going back to school!'

I'll swim with the fish off the
Great Barrier Reef
And eat spicy foods
And visit the pyramids,
I don't care, all I know is
I'm not going back to
School!

Harriet Gilchrist (10)

The World At Our Feet

If I could fly . . .
I would swoop, soar . . . sing
I would plunge through the clouds
If I could fly

If I could swim . . .
I would break the wild white foam
I would feel the freshness on my face
If I could swim

If I could run . . .
Wild and free, pushing the fresh air away
If I could I would scream, shout, laugh
If I could run

If we all work together we could all do those things
We are one big family
So the world should be
At our feet.

Hannah Potter (11)

The World At My Feet

I would love to be a horse rider
Famous for my skills
To win rosettes, cups and awards
The world would be at my feet

My horse would be called Midnight
A horse of pure and shining black
A snow-white star on her forehead
The perfect horse for me

I would love to own this horse
Of pure and shining black
For her to be mine, all mine
The world would be at my feet

I would love to win a special race
And millions and millions more
To have a whole cupboard of prizes
The world would be at my feet.

Yasmin Zahra

The World At Our Feet

Freedom is the life that I like,
Riding a scooter or even a bike.
Freedom is about being free,
Being as happy as can be.

Children should have their freedom and their play,
If you agree then you as well should have your say.
Children should be free,
As happy as they can possibly be.

Freedom is the chance,
To experience life to the full.
Freedom is to see the happiness,
Of what it is to be free.

Children should be allowed on their own,
Although such pressure grows from love.
To possibly take a mobile phone,
To be safe and free, exactly like me.

Freedom, freedom, freedom is what I like to see
And be totally free.

Jessica Letheren (10)

The World At Our Feet

Oh no, it's school tomorrow,
One day to finish my homework,
I've got to go to bed early,
Wake up when it's still dark.

I hate school!
I really wish I didn't have to go,
I just want to relax,
Laze about in the sun.

School is all about homework
And learning from A-Z,
The only good thing is,
That I'm in Year 6
And haven't long to go.

I absolutely hate school
And I wish I didn't have to go,
The first day always goes well,
It's the rest I worry about.

Zahra Ali (10)

When I'm Older

When I'm older
I'm doing a hard-working job
I'm going to be a vet
It will be great

I am

I'm going to be as clever
As a dog that has been trained
To look at cats
And puppies
And birds

I am

I have never tried hard before
It is too hard like trying to kill a lion
It is very, very hard

It is

It is very cold like me having nothing to wear
In the snow
Inside the checking room
It makes me colder every minute
It seems like cold ice!

It is

When I'm older I'm going to be as good as a puppy sleeping
I'm going to have lots of people coming to the vets
They're going to ask for me to help their pet
To be very, very healthy and good like a fish
This is my best dream, it will happen

It will.

Zoe Law (8)

I Want To Be

When I am older I want to . . .
Play for West Brom
And I want to play in goal
When I am older I want to be . . .
A really big star at football
I will be rich and have all the nice food, yum-yum

When I am older I want to be . . .
A big, big star at football
I shall take a swig of my drink
I will be diving in all the mud
When I am older I want to be . . .

Christy Kehoe

I Wonder Which One I'll Be

I'd probably be a spaceman
Walking on the clouds
Shooting water bombs down below
At the victims on the ground

But I'd definitely work in a sweet shop
Gobbling all the sweets
Laughing at the grannies
Eating mouldy meat

I could be an inventor
Inventing all day
Making a time machine
To send you all away

Or I could be a dentist
Checking people's teeth
Smelling their breath
I'd rather smell their feet

When I lie on my bed
And look up at the sky
I'll see the twinkly stars
As shiny as the sun
And I wonder what will I be?

Nathan Taylor (8)

When I Get A Job

When I get a job,
I'm gonna be
A person who rescues animals
With no home.
I'll rescue them.

Yes, I'll rescue them
And re-home them.

I'm gonna have
The biggest and the best building,
The cages are gonna be huge.

Yes, I'll rescue them
And re-home them.

I'm gonna feed them well,
Yes, I'll feed them well,
They'll have the comfiest bed ever made!

Rebecca Hammersley (8)

When I'm Doing Clothes

Lots of colours dark and bright
Cool by day, cool by night
Jazzy today, jazzy tonight
When I'm doing clothes

Mine is the fashion of today
After I've been working I say, 'Go and play,'
My day off is on Friday
When I'm doing clothes

I want lots of money
It will be as sweet as honey
The ink is kind of runny
When I'm doing clothes

I'll be feeling happy
When I'm doing clothes.

Phoebe Cook (8)

Planes

A nose of a plane
Short or long
Gotta be big
That's wrong

The speed of a plane
Very fast
600mph
That's fast

The height of a plane
Thousands of feet
Wow
That's gotta be high

The wings of a plane
Very big
Some even 50m long

The fuel of a plane
A lot of kg
Wow
This is so cool

The jets of a plane
Even faster
Wow (again)
This is even cooler.

Lee Walker (8)

When I'm A Footballer

When I grow up
I want to be a footballer
Playing for Wolves
And be a defender

I want to hear
The fans screaming
Their usual song

Goals! Goals! Goals!
Are fantastic
I want to score some
When I grow up

The players always
Have teamwork
No glory
Always teamwork.

Harry Dukes (8)

When I Become A TV Star

I'll be really sad if
I don't get this job
'Cause it's as bright as the sun

I'll be glad
If I'm on TV
Because I love it to bits
It's the best job ever

I'll be happy if
I get this job
'Cause it's been my biggest dream in the world

I'll be famous
If I do this
Probably
I'll buy myself a car or a house.

Jack Smith (8)

I Want To Be . . .

I want to be a superstar
So I can go round the world
I want to be a TV vet
So I can clean up sick animals

I want to be a soldier or a marine
So I can go on a speedboat
And explore the world

I want to be a multi-millionaire
So I can give to the poor
I want to be a model
And go to Paris in a limo
And see the Eiffel Tower.

Rebecca Dingwall (10)

My Hopes And Dreams

I hope I save the world
All the animals and all the people
I want to stop the poison too
In the future, I hope to be a pop star
In the future, I hope I can swim with dolphins
In the future, I hope to go on holiday
In the future, I hope I have a good life.

Alisha Crewe (10)

My Hopes And Dreams

In the future, I hope to swim with dolphins
Then I'll move to Southampton
I'll help all the sick animals that need help
I will save them whether they're big or small

In the future, I hope I can have a dolphin
And it will swim around all day
It will play and squirt as well
She will have rubbery skin.

Ruth Dalley (11)

The World At Our Feet

If I were rich
I'd buy my own sweet shop
And theme park too
I'd buy a country and rule that too
I'd make my own city
And be mayor of the town
I'd buy a school
And burn it to the ground
I'd make a rule
That everyone could drive
At the age of five
I'd bar all teachers from their job
Make them work at McDonald's
A big improvement to the world
That's what I'd do
If I were rich.

Peter Colhoun (10)

Untitled

If only I could get onto television,
Everyone seeing me,
Smiling nervously,
With people watching,
Lights, outfits, cameras and people clapping for me,
Singing the song for me,
Heart beats fast,
I finish the song,
As I wait for the results,
Say to myself is it me?
The light shines
And it is me!
That would be my dream.

Leona Quinn (10)

If I Were

If I were God
And ruled the world
Plus come down to Earth that would be good
I'd feed the hungry
Make everyone rich
Live in a big house
With forty servants
Have my own McDonald's and KFC
Plus Pizza Hut and Fun Factory
I'd have my own fair out the back
And all the candy that I want
I'd love the world and my family too
I'd be loyal to my friends like a good friend should.

Dearbhail Gillespie (10)

My Life

I would like to go to war, fight for my country,
Every day I dream about it and I hope and wish
That I was older

Or I wish I could be a spaceman, go to Pluto
Jump and fly because there is no gravity

Or why don't I be a superhero and drive a fancy car
My car would be a Ferrari and it would be red
And I'd have a big house with a jacuzzi

I would like to become a millionaire and give some to charity
Marry a nice girl and play with the children
And become even more rich

But what happens if I lose it all?
So I hope and wish that I get them.

Aaron Cleland (10)

I Want To Be . . .

Well I could . . .
Save a life by being a doctor
Or be an actor and win an Oscar
Be a musician and play in a band
Or be an explorer and discover new land

Be an archaeologist and find an ancient Greek pot
Or be a sailor and sail on a yacht
Be the President of the United States
Or work at a school where all the pupils are mates

Be a designer and work in fashion
Or be an artist with a great passion
But what I really want to do is just have fun
And think about all this when my growing up is done!

Verity Beckham (10)

I Wish To See The Future

I'd love to be an actress,
To see my name in the stars.
I'd love to help the poorer,
With diseases such as SARS.
The clothes and all the make-up,
They really are my style.
Even though I'm a country girl,
I know how dress is worthwhile.
I love acting at home and even more at school,
Acting is the best, I think it's really cool.
If I couldn't be an actress,
I love designing clothes,
I think I'd have a wardrobe full of my own things.
I'd feel like I had wings,
Others would be in envy
Of all my cool designs.
These are my wishes
To take me through my times.

Amy Stirling (10)

My Dream

Dream to work with animals,
To become a vet and look after animals.
To play with them and feed them too,
To make them feel better whenever they are ill.
To help them whenever they are in trouble.
Whenever an animal is alone, I will come and look after it
And if I'm not a vet, I will be a doctor.

Thomas Moore (10)

Supersonic Pilot

I want to be a pilot
And roll around the sky,
Fly at supersonic speed
And see the world flash by

I would speed past the oceans,
Streak across the sea
And if I go fast enough,
I'll be back in time for tea.

Samuel Bradley (10)

A Wrestler

I would be a wrestler,
A wrestler I would be,
A worldwide hero,
Prancing around the ring,
That's me!

I would enter in a stretch limo,
Come out with the championship belt,
I would be the best without a shadow of doubt,
That's me!

Lewis Lennane-Emm (10)

Living On A Desert Island

If I lived on a desert island,
I would lie in the blazing hot sun.
If I lived on a desert island,
I'm sure I would have some fun.

I would get some honey from the bees
And swing with the monkeys in the trees.
I would use coconuts for my milk
And leaves to wrap myself in silk.

If I lived on a desert island,
I would paddle in the sea.
If I lived on a desert island,
I hope the tribesmen would dance with me.

Laura Shirley (8)

Untitled

If I were rich I would jump up and down
Then share it all around
I would love to be rich, oh my, oh my

If I were rich I would see the world
And go past different streets
I would love to be rich, oh my, oh my

If I were rich I would buy a castle and have servants
With a bedroom nice and warm
So that's what I'd do if I were rich.

Ami Peaty (8)

Untitled

I had super power and I could kick and fight evil enemies
And people who robbed banks and robbed other places
I get ice breath and have laser power
I can fly really fast in the air when there's a crime
I am invisible as well and have other super powers.

Yasmin Lefevre (8)

Driving A Ferrari

D rumming engines
R eady to go
I nvisible Ferrari flying
V ibrating engine
I nside the car, steering wheel spinning
N obody beats our car
G oing very fast

A great car

F ast cars on the track
E veryone is cheering
R oaring engines
R ed Ferraris
A winner
R aise the trophy
I n the air.

Curtis Stokes (9)

Ferrari

F erraris go fast and crash
E lectric motors in them
R oaring engines
R acing along
A little crash and bash
R acing again
I won, I won a trophy.

Thomas Marfell (8)

Fighting Evil

F ighting evil, I'm really scared, I've got a sword but I'm scared.
I t's happening tonight, I'm scared, I've got the creeps I'm scared,
I'm still scared.
G oosebumps, I'm feeling goosebumps everywhere, my hands are
shaking terribly, I'm really scared.
H owever, I haven't got a gun or a disguise, I need to get them,
I'm very scared.
T onight is very close, it's too scary, I don't want to go,
I'm really, really scared.
N ow it's time to go, my dad could go instead, I'm not going now.
G etting my dad to do it for me will be great, I know I'm still scared.

E vil, he's evil, an evil giant, he's got muscles, I'm really scared.
V ery scary he is, 'Dad, can you do it for me, please?' 'Yes,
I 'll do it for you, son, I'm not scared!'
L ots of thanks Dad, thank you!

Katie Wilson (8)

Ferrari

F ast zooming cars
E ach car is really fast
R eally, really fast cars
R acing track is where Ferraris lap
A fter a race back on the road
R acing is Ferrari's favourite thing
I saw Ferraris on the road, racing, zoom!

Joshua Walker (8)

All The Different Things I Would Like To Do

I will go to Australia and be a crocodile hunter
And work in an Australian zoo.

I wish I had super powers
And then I will help the world.

I wish I was a racing driver
So I can drive a F1 Ferrari.

I will like to be a football player
So I can play for Arsenal.

I would like to be an army man
So I can use a gun and protect the world.

I want to be a policeman
So I can drive a police car.

Thomas Lea (9)

Playing For Southampton Or Real Madrid

In my future I would like to . . .
Play football for Southampton
Or Real Madrid

I want to play for Southampton
Because I support Southampton
And I support Real Madrid.

Luke Wrixon (9)

My Dream

I would like to be a vet
To zoom around all day long
I wish I was a singer
So I could earn money
I would like to help the animals and run
Chasing the wild cats to give them their jabs
When I get home I'll bring a cat home
A wild one.

Briony Luscombe (9)

If Only I . . .

If only I was a lawyer,
I'd live in a cottage if I could.
Have my nan back,
If only I could,
Live up to 100,
Wow, that would be good.

If only I could stop the wars,
Have a family too,
Maybe be the Queen,
Even maybe a manager of a shop,
If only I could.

If only I could save those poor people,
The woods and the animals in it
And recycle all the things we don't want,
That would be good.

If only I could leave all my troubles behind me,
Then I could maybe be an author,
If I could go to art school, draw cartoons there,
If only I could.

Paige Davies (9)

I Would Like . . .

I would like to be a pilot flying in the air
I would like a good life, before I leave the world forever
It will be the best holiday I could give my family
I would like a nice car for my family and a van would be good too
I would like to be a very good carpenter.

Ben Taylor (9)

Great Mystery

Oh how I want to be a TV presenter
And see the ways of life
To see how Mother Nature works
With animals and mammals
Reptiles and birds

I want to know how it's going
Knowing how life is a great mystery
How it works in this way
How far I go
I want to know life's great mystery.

Charles Barlow (9)

All The Things I Would Do

If I won the lottery . . .
I would go and swim with the dolphins
For hours and hours and hours

If I won the lottery . . .
I would help the poor people
By giving them my money
If I lived on a lovely desert island
I would go swimming every day

When I am older . . .
I would like to be a famous person
Looking after the world

If I was a vet . . .
I would be looking after lots of pets
If I was an entertainer
I would entertain the world.

Amey Coombes (9)

Fire Vs Fire

I would be a firefighter
Saving people
So I would dive into fire
To save the day
Doing right rather than wrong
Never giving up
Always doing my best

Always facing my fears
Always looking at the bright side
I would fight for freedom
The world and the Queen.

Brandon Wynn (9)

My Dreams

All of my dreams feel really real,
Oh how I wish they were.

An artist is what I want to be,
Paint the world to make it look free.

Save the world,
So no evil will be in it.

Have a brilliant education,
So I can be smart.

Be an actress,
So I can win lots of prizes.

Make sure my family is OK,
All the time.

Be really famous,
So that I can go on lots of holidays.

Rebecca Paveley (10)

My Dreams

I would like to be a secret agent
And run around,
The best thing of all
Is not making a sound.

I would like to have 1000 dogs,
The worst thing of all
Would be having slimy frogs.

I would like to have a cat called Mark,
The best thing of all
Would be going to the park.

Jodie Austin (9)

My Dreams

I would like to be a butcher
To give people meat for them to eat
I would like to be a professional football player
For West Ham Utd or Arsenal

I would like to be a secret agent
Saving the people and having lethal weapons

I would like to be an Australian zookeeper
To see pandas eating bamboo.

Richard Mundy (9)

A Perfect World

I would like to stop cruelty in the world
Because people get scared
When some person hurts them
And burns them

I would like to give peace to the world
And stop the war
And be a teacher to teach people
And tell them about how they can stop the wars

I would give holidays to people
That never have been on holiday
All their lives before

I would like to live in a peaceful world
Because it would be nice to have a quiet world to live in

I would like to help the old people
With anything I can and I would help people to learn.

Katrina Annetts (10)

My Future

In my future
I would like to become
A famous dirt bike rider
And a famous football player
For England and Man U.

Jonathan Newham (10)

Hopes And Dreams

I would like to be an actor
And be on TV.

I'd like to become a sailor
And sail the seven seas.

I'd like to be a pilot in a plane
And fly around in the air.

I'd like to be a soldier and fight for peace
I would like to keep this world safe from any danger.

Jay Pritchard (9)

Wishes

I wish I could be an athlete
Running like the wind
Jumping like the horses
And be as fast as a cheetah

I wish I could be a pop star
Singing to the world
Making up tracks
And being on live stage

I wish I could own every park
To slide down slippy slides
To go swishing through the trees
To go down water rides

I wish I could give peace
To help the young
To help the old
And to give peace to God

I wish I could help the poor
To give them food
To give them energy
To make them strong.

Sophie Jocelyn (9)

If Only

If only I was an athlete,
I would run as fast as can be,
I would run and jump on my bar,
I would be as silly as can be.

If only I could help the poor,
Then I would be so special,
I would give them food and water
And make them feel at home.

If only I could leave all my troubles behind me,
I would be so happy and not so sad.

Harley Luckhurst (9)

Great Dreams

I'd like to be an ice cream woman
And have a shiny van
And make lots of children happy
And make loads of money

I'd like to learn a lot
And be an artist teacher
I like drawing creatures
And make loads of pictures

I'd like to be rich
To go on holiday
It's nice and sunny
To play out in the day

I'd like to have super powers
To save the people around the world
And make them safe
And make them be brave.

Jade Long (9)

My Hopes And Dreams

I hope I will get a dolphin
That splashes in the sea,
All day long it's splash, splash, splash.

My dreams are to go and live in Lanzarote,
So we can laugh and play,
Go swimming every day.

My hopes are to be rich
And have a boyfriend and live happy in a palace,
With my mum and dad and friends and family.

My dreams are to be a pop star
And have lots of friends
And live in the United States.

My hopes are to go on holiday,
Have fun on the beach and in the sea,
To go swimming every day.

Jessica Hoppe (10)

Elephant

In the future I hope I will have an elephant
I will slide down his trunk like a slide
And eat nuts with him every day.

Zoey Fernandes (10)

My Dream

If I had a choice to work anywhere,
I would get a job at a zoo!
Gallop with the horse and ride on the ponies,
Playing with the elephants and there's other stuff to do.

I would wash the elephants every week,
I would race the cheetahs and they would win,
I'd clean flamingo beaks,
I'd jump in the water with the hippos and go for a swim.

Lucy Jones (10)

The Game

There once was a flame,
When I was in a game,
When we had a goal,
We made a massive hole,
The manager was sacked,
Because we weren't back,
Once I was down the side,
I crossed and someone hit it wide,
Our team howled,
Because of a fake foul,
The final whistle blew,
We had beat the blues.

Ross Purfit (10)

My Future

In the future
I would like to be
A famous footballer
For England
And Man United.

Nick Scott (10)

If
(Based on 'If' by Rudyard Kipling)

If you are sensible to not take drugs,
I rely on you to say no.

If your friends drink alcohol in their teens,
You will know not to.

If someone is being hateful,
Don't be hateful back.

If your friends persist to steal from shops,
Please don't copy.

Yours is the Earth and everything that's in it,
And - which is more - you'll be a woman my girl.

Amy-Louise Collier & Louise Sleeman (10)

If . . .
(Based on 'If' by Rudyard Kipling)

If you can ignore them when they call you names,
If you can work hard even when people are noisy,
If you can share even if people are your enemies,
If you can study hard at home even if your brother annoys you,
If you can go on a diet even if you are tempted to have sweets,
If you can do your A levels even though you make mistakes.

Joe Hewitt (10)

If
(Based on 'If' by Rudyard Kipling)

If you are able to not fight back,
The enemy will leave you alone,
If you can walk with such a heavy backpack,
They shall deeply drop their tone.

If you can talk without raising the voice,
You shall not be a disaster,
If they gave you a free choice,
Would you be the world's master?
Yours is the Earth and everything that's in it
And - which is more - you'll be a man my son.

Aaron Mantle (10)

If

(Based on 'If' by Rudyard Kipling)

If you can say no to smoking,
While everyone is taking a puff.
If you can stay sober,
While everyone is drunk.
If you can stay out of trouble,
While everyone is in it.
If you take drugs
You will feel the pain.
Yours is the Earth and everything that's in it,
And - which is more - you'll be a man my son.

James Webster & Danny Vallance (10)

If

(Based on 'If' by Rudyard Kipling)

If you wear your car seatbelt
Although your friends do not want to,
That's good, because you must,
Then you will stay alive.
If you wear your car seatbelt,
Although your friends refuse to,
That's best for you because
You need to avoid those accidents.

If you can stay sober,
When other people can't,
Then you are doing the right thing,
When other people aren't.
If you can refuse drugs,
When your friends can't,
Then you are very strong.
Yours is the Earth and everything that's in it
And what's more, you'll be a woman, my girl!

Susanna von Hallwyl & Naomi Miller (10)

If

(Based on 'If' by Rudyard Kipling)

If you can refuse drugs
Even though you are high
If you can avoid alcohol
Even when your friends are drunk
If you can save money
Even though your mates steal
Yours is the Earth and everything that's in it
And - which is more - you'll be a man, my son!

Adam Loveday & Jonathan Tinkler (10)

If

(Based on 'If' by Rudyard Kipling)

If you can keep away from drugs
When all around you are being tempted

If you can keep away from temptation
Despite your friends willing you on

If you can turn and walk away from trouble
Yet still hold your head up proud when friends are jeering you on

If you can strive to do your best
Even when you find it tough and others find it easy

If you can fill each day with happiness
And yours is the Earth and everything that's in it
And - wake up to laughter when others are not
Yours is the Earth and everything that's in it
And - which is more - you'll be a man, my son!

Michael Glasson & Karl Jeffery (10)

If
(Based on 'If' by Rudyard Kipling)

If you don't steal
When your friends do
If you refuse drugs
Even though your friends take them,
If your friend is in hospital
Because drugs made him crash in his car,
If you wear your seatbelt
It won't happen to you,
You will feel much safer
And you'll be a man, my son.

Rory Abbey & Scott Jackson (10)

If
(Based on 'If' by Rudyard Kipling)

If nicotine can be your enemy whilst your friend thinks it's great,
If people put you down yet you still stand up tall,
If a dream can be your aim but not be your obsession,
If you can beat drugs once you have already began with your mates.

If you do not drink when your friends are drunk,
If you can wear your seatbelt whilst others make fun of you,
If you do not take a penny when your mates rob a bank,
If you do not drink and drive when your friends don't even have their licence,
If you can tell the truth when others always lie.

Your Earth is yours and everything in it
And - which is more - you will be a man my son!

Joseph Dunford & Robert Binns (10)

If

(Based on 'If' by Rudyard Kipling)

If you can never tell a lie or spread one
If you meet new friends
Don't let down your old ones
If people are upset, don't make it worse
If your friends are thieves
Don't be a thief yourself
If you can refuse drugs
When your friends are taking them
If you can ignore bad behaviour
While others are being bad
Yours is the Earth and everything that's in it
And - which is more - you'll be a man my son.

Stuart Cull & Timothy Anderson-Emm (10)

If

(Based on 'If' by Rudyard Kipling)

If you could change the thoughts of others,
Don't change them for yourself,
If you could change time,
Don't change it for yourself,
If people around you are acting,
Try and be yourself,
If drugs are your friends' destiny,
Try to steer yourself from temptation,
Yours is the Earth and everything that's in it
And - what's more - you'll be a man my son.

James Docherty (11) & Ben Lister (10)

If
(Based on 'If' by Rudyard Kipling)

If you can make your bed and sleep in it
And not complain once

If you can get untangled from
Your web of lies

If you can tell the truth
While others stand in shadows

If you can say no to drugs
While others around you take them

If you can resist temptation
At its highest point

If you can be polite
While others around you are rude

Yours is the world and everything that's in it
And - which is more - you'll be a woman, my girl.

Kerry Blyth & Victoria Moore-Morton (10)

If
(Based on 'If' by Rudyard Kipling)

If you wear lipstick and make-up
And never stroll or strut.
If you wear designer clothes,
Don't count yourself as the best.

If others wear the latest trend,
But you don't, don't have tantrums like a child.
Yours is the Earth and everything that's in it
And - which is more - you'll be a woman, my girl.

Jasmine Simon (10)

If

(Based on 'If' by Rudyard Kipling)

If you can keep your head and stay calm
While your friends drown their sorrows by taking drugs
If you can run and not look back behind you
While your friends are stupid and become thugs
If you can wear your seat belt
While others don't
You will be safe
While others won't
But most importantly you will be a man, my son.

Ashley Davies (11) & Anthony Robinson (10)

If

(Based on 'If' by Rudyard Kipling)

If you can ignore the drugs
Yet other people take them
If you can wear a seat belt
Although your friends don't bother
If you can avoid smoking
While other people don't even care
If you can have a pint or two
You're surely to get drunk

Yours is the Earth and everything that's in it
And - which is more - you'll be a woman, my girl.

Jessica Dyer & Georgia-Rae Tryhorn (10)

Untitled

I would like to see happy kids and grown-ups too
I would drive around the world and make everyone happy
I would help the poor and I would destroy evil
I would give the poor homes
I would win the lottery and buy a mansion
I'd give the world peace.

Marc (9)

Pop Star

P opping on my stereo
O h my speakers are popping now
P op! Pop! Pop!

S tarting a music career, yo, yo, yo!
T aking all my CDs, giving them to my mates
A nd I'm at No 1
R ap! Rap! Rap!

Kieron Malik (10)

Manchester United

M anchester United are the best team in the world
A nyone you want to buy
N ever be a city, Arsenal, Liverpool or any other team, support Man U

U p and down to the toilet
N ever bite your nails because United won't lose
I wish I played for United
T owards the net
E at Jaffa Cakes before the match
D own the wing Ronaldo goes.

Zak Butterworth-Joyce (10)

Rich And Poor

R ich children grow up spoilt and selfish,
I nside mansions are their grand possessions,
C hauffeurs drive these people everywhere,
H ow happy rich people are!

P ennies are what some poor people lack,
O nly rich people they envy!
O nly money is what they want,
R oofless are some people's houses!

Emily Walsh (10)

Pop Idol

P op stars singing, that's what I would like to do
O h gosh, I've got through an audition,
P rancing around, waiting for some news.

I n and out of rooms, feeling dead excited,
D ad is coming to pick me up in his new car,
O ver the bridge, going back to Pop Idol,
L ondon here I come.

Abigail Grimmett (10)

Rich

R iding around in a McClaren F1
I n and out the clothes shop
C hildren in my swimming pool
H appy holidays in the sun.

Lauren Griffiths (11)

Save The World!

When I save Earth,
I'll have a team
Of the best robots
I have ever had.

Evil will die,
Good will live,
Light rocks!
Darkness is doomed,
Hopes are possible!

Saving animals,
Helping the environment!
Tree cutters beware,
No pollution allowed!
Super Junaid is here,
I'm saving the world,
Darkness dies!

Junaid Mir (10)

My Dream

In twenty years' time
I will cross the line
Of the athletic stadium
I will run for miles
Miles and miles
So this is my dream
To be in the team
I will be a beginner
And the winner.

Chloe Waugh (9)

Star

A star is what I want to be,
Lots of people looking at me,
Performing everywhere on stage,
I would be a star at any age,
People coming from far and near,
They would come every year,
So I really want to be a star
And I want to go far.

Paige Storer (9)

Pop Star!

I wish to be a pop singer like Ashanti
Singing on the shiny stage,
I want it to be on a CD
With words on the page.
I would like it to be my dream come true,
If you were a pop star everyone will love you.
You might even sing far up to the stars.

Lorraine Terry (9)

My Dream Is Being A Pop Star

My dream might come true,
My dream is new.
But hey who knows?
I might sing in the snow,
Would I get fans
And people even driving in vans?
When's the time?
And that's my rhyme.

Homan Cheung (9)

Me, Dad And The Holiday Storm

Holidays are so much fun
Lying bathing in the sun

But when I went to sunny Spain
It suddenly began to rain

We were splashing in the sea
Being as happy as can be

When it suddenly began to pour
And everybody swam to shore

When Dad and I reached the sand
We grabbed the bags, one in each hand

And ran towards our private villa
Where I laid my head upon my pillow

Suddenly bright lightning flashed
And seconds later thunder crashed

It rained and rained, it never stopped
You'd think an ocean had just dropped

And just as quickly as it started
Those nasty clouds, they just departed

Bursting through came the blazing sun
Back down to the beach I began to run

And as I reached the glistening shore
It suddenly began to pour . . . again!

Katie Fisher (10)

I Wish I Could

I wish I could be in the police force
I wish I could be a policeman
I wish I could fly to America
I wish I could drive a police car
I wish I could fight all day with the smallest toy gun there is
I wish I could make the world a safer place
I wish I could fight the bad
I wish, I wish.

Abid Ramzan (9)

My Pet Dolphin And My Pet Horse

My pet dolphin jumped out of the sea.
My pet horse jumped over the gate.
My pet dolphin got loved by me.
My pet horse got hugged by me.
My pet dolphin swam by me.
My pet horse sat by me.
My pet dolphin got kissed by me.
My pet horse got kissed by me.
I love my pets and they love me.
My dolphin and my horse.

Dawn Ringrose (9)

When I Am Older

When I am older it would be nice to have super powers
I'd stop all bad
And not let anyone be sad
I'd save almost everyone
When someone comes with a bomb
No one would ever die
If they did, I'd hit the sky
When bad is defeated
The world would be a better place
Everyone will have a happy face.

Sarah Howard (9)

I Wish I Was In The Police Force

I wish I was in the police force
I'd have to take a training course
Then I'll have chases
Because of street racers
With my police car
I'll go really far
Then I'd say, 'Bring out the stinger'
And then I'd switch on my ringer.

Amir Meziane (9)

My Dream

I wish, I wish in 20 years
I want to become rich
And then travel right round the world
In a Ferrari
I would like to go to Australia
Hollywood, Africa
Then anywhere else.

Ben Gallagher (9)

I Wish, I Wish

I wish, I wish
I was a pop star
That sang the night away
Maybe like Avril Lavigne
I don't know anyway
I might fly around the world
Or go to Hollywood
If I don't get to be a pop star
I'll still be in the neighbourhood.

Lauren Rayment (9)

Saving The World

Be the best than the last
Kill the bad, be the lad
Help mankind than behind
To have good powers
For strong people
But help poor countries
For their need
Give them the water that's clean
Stop the wars so nobody gets injured
Fly to space
And gain in pace
I'll wish and wish
Until that day comes.

Andrew Dicorato (9)

I Am A Spy

I am a spy
I like saving the world
People like me and I like them
I like to watch out in my secret, secret den
I work with a man called Ken
But Ken doesn't know that I have a secret, secret den.

Jamie Booth (9)

Untitled

I want to be a pop star
And dance my little heart out

If I was a pop star
I would even shout to let feelings out

I would have something to do with fame
They would all know my name

Always try my best to try and impress

Right here, right now, my dream shall come true
But I would need someone to work with, how about you?

Mica Howarth (9)

I Will Become Rich

I wish I could become rich and buy a mansion
My friends would become jealous, I say jealous!
People would make me mad
So I would get security to chase them off my land
They might get away, they might get caught
But ever on I would be happy forever.

Jak Collinge (9)

Artist

When I grow up I will be the famous artist who ever lived in the world
I will win all the art competitions in the world
I will win the trophy and I will be the most artistic boy who ever lived.

Oliver Sewell (9)

Holidays

Holidays are so much fun,
Getting browner in the sun,
On the plane and in the pool,
Six whole weeks without any school,
From making castles in the sand
And watching grains fall through your hand,
To splashing through the waves at sea
And catching fish to eat for tea,
Everyone enjoys a holiday,
Time to relax or so they say,
All the memories will be mine,
So back to school until next time.

Samantha Donald (10)

My Dream Weekdays

Monday, went to school and sorted the hall out
Tuesday, went to school and did some maths
Wednesday, went to school and did some literacy
Thursday, went to school and did some IT
Friday, went to school and did some games
Saturday, went to football
Sunday, staying home and getting ready.

Bryn Roberts (10)

It's Really Frustrating Trying To Think Of A Poem

It's really frustrating trying to think of a poem,
    When you don't know what to write,
It's really frustrating trying to think of a poem,
    When it keeps you awake all night.

It's really frustrating trying to think of a poem,
    When your sister's acting the fool,
It's really frustrating trying to think of a poem,
    When you've just come home from school.

It's really frustrating trying to think of a poem,
    It drives you round the bend,
It's really frustrating trying to think of a poem,
    But I've finally reached the end.

Oliver Muir (10)

The Spy Poem

A spy is a good thing to do
Why you might say
I don't know
I know I want to be a spy
Because I like adventures in other places
In my heart a spy will always be
A spy is the best in my heart.

Merryn Edwards (7)

One Day . . .

One day I was writing a poem for hullabaloo!
When I felt that feeling like I needed the loo!
I started to grow till I felt like a I was fifty-foot tall,
I was even bigger than Humpty Dumpty's wall.
I went to a footy match, of course I scored a goal,
But I didn't fall into any little holes.
I wonder if I trod on some sheep,
Are they all in a heap?
I wonder if Mum's gone crazy?
I wonder if Mum's all sad?
Now I sit and think is my bruv saying his maths poem,
This is how it goes,
5 times 1 = 5,
The number five is alive,
10 counting sticks to count,
But I don't know the amount,
With a smart teacher to teach
And know I want the world at my feet.

Emily Heartfield (8)

The Dancing Queen

First the drum starts the beat,
Then the guitars start joining in,
Then the crowd start clapping, whistling,
All the noise added to the din.

Then out she comes,
In her lilac jeans,
Not forgetting the blue satin top,
Out comes the dancing queen.

Jumping up and down,
Spinning on the spot.
Flipping through the air,
Doing what's hot.

The final move she makes,
Is the splits,
When I grow up,
I want to dance to all the great hits!

Rebecca Tomsett (11)

Huge Mansion

When I'm grown up I want to live in
A huge mansion, which thin
People would die for and fat
People would diet for.
Mad about cat people would miaow for,
Dog people would bark like mad for.

When I'm grown up I want to live in
A huge mansion, me and Emma,
My best friend.
We'll each marry a husband,
We'll earn lots of money 'cause we'll be so clever,
We'll live there and be friends forever and ever.

Alice Shield (8)

If I Could Fly . . .

I'd soar through the air
With the clouds skimming my back
And the golden sun smiling
My grin wouldn't fade
As the birds sang sweetly
I'd watch the world below
And see the cars like multicoloured beetles
And the people like ants
The wonderful dipping feeling in my stomach
So soothing, as I thought this would never end.

Caitlin Walker (8)

Where Am I?

Soft sand, gold and brown,
The red-hot sun shining down,
The bright blue sea, sweeping at my feet,
A little bird going tweet, tweet
Really tall coconut trees
A nice, quiet, gentle breeze
Why am I
Staring at the sky?
I'm lost on a desert island.

Rachel Grieb (10)

World At My Feet

War alarms going off, noise from the mayor,
People the world over saying a prayer,
Draining damp over coves in a small hospice,
Animals dreaming, distant people screaming,
Our lives drawing to a close, as we slow down,
How can we help drain the sorrow, help the poor,
Give to the needy, stop the war?
Ask God more and more to help the world for soon it will die.

Sophie Clark (11)

What A Dancer!

'What a dancer,
What a star.'
Winning contests
Near and far
Whirling, twirling,
Pointing toes,
How her cup collection grows and grows!
Leaping, prancing, skipping
And dancing.

Justine Porter (10)

Homework

Come home from school,
Homework is there,
Pages are blank and
My book is bare.

Stomp up the stairs
And slam the door,
Lie on my bed and try
Some more.

I've got it now,
Here we go,
Get my pen
And away we flow.

Victoria Seales (10)

Over The Hills And Far Away

When I was young and had no sense
I bought a fiddle for eighteen pence
And the only tune that I could play
Was 'Over the hills and far away'.

Sorcha Convery (9)

To Be An Actress

A n actress is what I want to be
C an I make my dream come true?
T o some people it may be crazy
R ealise they might say
E veryone has a dream, but don't waste your life away
S o I want to be an actress
S o I want to be a star

O h I don't think it's crazy
S ome people may
C ome on I say, I could be one day
A n actress on the stage
R ealise is what I think

S ome people are
I n films and shows
N o one should give up their dream
G o out into the world
I 'm going to try
N o one thinks it's right saying lines for a living
G ive it a try, I would.

Katherine Dansie (9)

Saving The World

Once when I was walking to school,
I saw a big crocodile crossing the road,
All of a sudden my eyes did something funny
And the crocodile had turned into honey.
That night, when I was at my house,
My mum's body was on fire!
I touched it and then it was back to normal, as I decided.
When I was at school next day,
The teacher turned into an alien,
Nobody noticed or even cared,
Until I was in the air,
Whacking it with a broom!
That night when I was in my room,
I opened the window and I flew out the room,
I came down for breakfast,
The very next morning,
My mum said,
'Oh my, how strange, make sure you
Take that crocodile out before school!'

Kate Morris (10)

I Wish Upon A Star

I gazed through my bedroom window at the twinkling wishing star
Up in the velvet night sky stretching so far
I reached out to the wishing star and shouted, 'Please may
You make all my wishes come true in a big way,'
I wish for smiles instead of tears
I wish for peace instead of war
I wish for gentleness instead of violence
I wish for food instead of famine
I wish for honesty instead of crime
I wish for love instead of cruelty
I wish for sunshine and rain instead of floods and droughts
I wish for safe inventions and discoveries instead of dangerous creations
I wish for more giving, sharing and caring instead of thoughtlessness
I wish for togetherness and friendship instead of selfishness and hate
Then all of a sudden, I heard a cluck, cluck
Oh dear! It was my good old cluck-coo alarm clock
Who did wake me up with a startle one early morning
Never mind, if it was all a dream
Maybe it will all come true one day!

Tanuvi Ethunandan (9)

My Dream

Car designing is my dream,
I think cars are the best vehicle on Earth,
Spare time is normally car designing,
Dad has had a lot of cars, a little mini to a big jeep,
The jeep he has now is a Landrover Freelander
The most amazing invention by far.

Jordan Peverley (9)

My Dreams

I want to be an author
And write lots of books.
Spending all day imagining things
And not really doing any work.

I'd like to win an award,
For one of my fabulous plots.
To be walking down the street and hearing someone say,
'Isn't she the girl who won that children's award?'
Gosh wouldn't that be cool!

My teachers say I should be an author
And I totally agree,
One day you might be reading a book
And the author of it could be me!

Lauren Ismail (11)

On The Run

Here I live in a polluted city
Dirty streets
What a pity!
It's hard to breathe fresh air
Because the fumes are everywhere
Now I'm in a noisy plane
Getting out of the fast lane
To a sandy beach
Miles away
Out of reach

All I see is a coconut tree
Clear white sand
Upon the open land
I'm diving down beneath the ocean
The fish are swimming in slow motion
Wait a second, could it be
There's a cleaner world beneath the sea!

Henry Fabre (10)

One Day

I'd love to be a pop star
I'd love to sing and dance
I'd love to have the microphone
I'd never miss that chance

I'd love to step on stage
I'd love to write some songs
I'd love to be in a studio
And sing out all my songs

One day . . .

Hannah Tyler (10)

What To Wish For?

One day I saw a genie,
Sitting on the ground,
He said I'd get three wishes,
Worth a million pound!

My first of the wishes was easy,
I wished that I could fly
Around the moon, above the clouds,
Up in the dark blue sky.

When that wish was granted,
I didn't know what to do,
I was having a lot of trouble,
Thinking of wish two.

All of a sudden it came to me,
I was going to wish for world peace,
Then everyone would be such good friends,
Just like in the film 'Grease'.

After that my luck ran out,
I couldn't think of a thing,
Then an idea popped into my head,
I wished that I could sing!

Sarah Bolt (11)

If I Was Rich . . .

If I was rich I'd drive a sports car,
I might one day be a famous pop star!
I'd buy valuable clothes and shoes.
When I go to a party, I'll know the right moves!
I will have a servant that will serve me ice cream,
Maybe I can have a netball team.
I'd buy an enormous house that was really pretty,
I'll get a beautiful pet kitty!

One day I would travel on a first class aeroplane around the world,
Sometimes I would style my hair straight or curled.
I'd be a presenter on 'Top of the Pops',
My own security guard will just be like the cops!
On sunny days I will jump in my swimming pool,
When I go somewhere royal I'll drive in my limousine, cool!
When I wake up, surprise! surprise!
What I dreamt about is there before my eyes!

Baveena Heer (8)

Pet Shop

Walking down the rows and rows,
Looking for a pet,
But what to have,
I could have a rabbit, dog or a guinea pig,
There's one I like, how much? £100,
I'll never get a pet,
Wait, there's more,
My mum is coming, time to go,
'Mum, I have found one, over here, a dog.'
'Good, how much?' asked mum,
'£100!' I called back,
We got it, his name is Nessie!

Charlotte Thomas (9)

My Dream

If that was a squirrel
I would be
Or maybe a dolphin
Under the sea
I could be a snake
No, that is hardly me

Maybe a dog
On my four legs I'd bound
Sure I could be a mole
I would dig a great mound
Just maybe a hedgehog
My spikes scare off enemies I found

My dream is saving the world
In our world there are so many creatures
So many animals are in danger
The miracle of nature is one of our many features
Some animals are close to extinction
So please let us listen to our teachers.

Hattie Le Gresley (10)

One Day I Want To Join The Navy

I am a junior in the sea cadets
There's lots to learn
From the ranks above
Teaching me what they know
I can't wait to see a Navy day show

When I'm sailing in a Walker Bay
The wind picks up and I'm away
Across the river, the ripples flowing
I'm so excited, my cheeks are glowing

Now down to the serious stuff
Learning drill and standing still
Tying knots, first aid and practising
For Remembrance Parade

Here comes my first Royal Navy inspection
Quite nervous meeting the Lt Commander
But very honoured to be selected
To call evening colours
That's not what I expected

The more I go, the more I learn
And makes me more determined to get on well
One day I will join the Navy.

Aaron Milne-Redhead (10)

When I Become Rich

When me and my family
Become millionaires
I'm going to buy a mansion
That'll have loads of stairs

It'll be the biggest in the world
It's going to be so cool!
It will have its own fitness gym
And a swimming pool

My maids will have hi-tech brooms
To sweep after me
When I'm in one of my one hundred and one rooms

It'll be open to the public
And they'll have to pay
Nine pounds ninety-nine
To use the pool for a day.

Natalie Mckenzie-Buksh (10)

My Dream Of A Little Mouse

I am a little mouse
Who lived in a big house
I always want to play on a sunny day
I am brown, I want to wear a crown

I have two round ears with some brown hairs
There is a cat called Slaybour
Who is my next-door neighbour

He likes to play catch with me
So he knocks on my door and
Waves his paw
But he is the best friend that I've ever had.

Priyanthy Elangovan (10)

Pop Idol

P op is great
O n the stage, performing on Pop Idol is great
P eter, Nicky, Simon and Foxy are judges

I know Simon is evil
D oh! Gareth did not win!
O h no, Will won
L ike Gareth, I do because he is great!

Abi Rose Braithwaite (8)

Pop Idol

P op Idol is the best
O h yes Gareth Gates might win
P eter is a judge

I heard Gareth and Will sing on Pop Idol
D oh! Will won Pop Idol
O f all the pop idols I think Gareth is the best
L ove in the air on Pop Idol.

Sophie Morris (8)

Save The World

Terrorism, hunger and war
Is something not permitted by law
I would save everything and everyone
Mankind would be content
No fighting, no bullying
No terrorism within
This terrorism would go to waste
War would stop
This pain and hunger
Would not exist
Now this violence must stop
Come everyone
'Have a go'.

Julieann Lewis (9)

Hopes

H opes, everyone has them!
O h, how can you not have a hope?
P opular ones are being rich, being magic,
E ven being a superhero who saves the world,
S o remember, everyone has a hope!

Richard Winter (9)

Future

Going for gold all the time
Don't let yourself down
Dreams do come true in life
The world is all yours
Reach for the moon all the time!
Be a pop idol
Lead the way all the time.

Matthew Simpson (9)

Poem Of The World

I hope to be a soldier so I can shoot my enemies
I think I would be good as a soldier
If they asked me to do something
I would say, 'Roger that!'

Maybe in the future I could be a chef
Because I could cook spaghetti Bolognese
Yum-yum, in the future I might be a chef
Maybe, maybe not

I hope to be a wrestler so I can get a lot of money
And also I would be evil and slam people to the ground.

Nathan Ferrier (9)

The World Cup Final 2004

Crowds gather together under the dark night sky,
Players shake hands ready for the final to begin.
Everyone is in position and the whistle blows,
Striker versus striker, who will win the game?

Foul by the Brazilian captain results in a penalty,
The crowd is tense, will he score?
Eight steps back are taken and then . . . goal!
Straight into the top right corner.

Brazil kick-off yet again,
With a roar, the crowd have gone wild!
The ball is in the penalty box, passes the keeper,
On the volley another goal is scored!

What a fantastic goal,
England are on a roll.
But charging down the pitch come Brazil,
About to strike but the whistle blows.

Brazil are really fired up now,
Another goal must be scored,
A cross comes in and heads straight into England's net,
Wow! A come-back, Brazil are back in the game.

Brazil now have only a few minutes to score,
A free kick crossed in the box just as the whistle blows.
England have won the World Cup!
He crowd rise with a deafening cheer.

Adam Dawson (10)

The Bengal Tigers

The Bengal tigers live joyfully,
In their home full of freedom.
The baby cubs fight gleefully together,
While the adults lie in the shade.

Their lovely, bushy, soft fur,
Coloured with orange and black.
Their big, yellow, gloomy eyes,
Gaze with a deadly stare.

They live in one hot country,
In the western sights of India.
At home on prairie plains,
Under the eastern sun.

Narinder Atwal (10)

Dreaming Of Dolphins

I would like to swim with dolphins
And go under the sea.
It is bright and colourful,
It's a wonderful place to be.

I'd grab onto the thick grey skin,
As they twist and twirl all the time.
They dive into the ocean depths,
Swimming with great ease.

I'd watch them swim really fast,
While catching fish,
They'd quickly dart about,
Scooping up their lunch.

Elizabeth Boiling (10)

My Hopes And Dreams

M y dream is to be a teacher!
Y es but don't say that I will be heard of the school!

H orrible moments at times but it's the best way to make them
    get on with the work
O n the day I become a teacher I will get to know names
    and more names!
P lay times they will not want to go out because I will be nice
    and the tasks will be great!
E xciting moments at art and maths!
S ome names and people I will get mixed up with!

A ctivities at golden time will be busy!
N othing wrong because I will be there for help!
D ifferent feelings every day!

D ifferent tasks to complete, but I will enjoy marking them!
R emember if there was no school you would be bored without me!
E xplaining will be easy because I won't be nervous!
A class likes art and maths will come to me!
M y classroom will be bright!
S uper fun, I am the teacher to have!

Samantha Thomson Naylor (10)

Going Pro

When I grow up I want to be a footballer
And save every shot and score every goal
I want to be number one

When I grow up I want to be a BMX stunt rider
And get loads of points for tricks and jumps

When I grow up I want to be a motorbiker
And win every race and win every cup
I want to be number one

When I grow up I want to be a sports car designer
And make really fast cars to break the world record

When I grow up I want to be a PlayStation 2 game designer
And get lots of money for making good games

When I grow up I want to be a squash player
And beat the world's best
I want to win every tournament

Now I am back in my seat at school
Waiting for this to happen!

Alex Valenzuela (9)

Jobs

I want to be a scientist
And a very good one,
I'll see and study the sun,
Oh! I want to be a scientist.

I want to be an artist
And invent new styles,
And if I do that I'll travel for miles,
Oh! I want to be an artist.

I want to be a doctor
And I'll help people as well,
My fame will still propel,
Oh! I want to be a doctor.

I want to be an athlete
I will go for gold,
And I will not stop until I am old,
Oh! I want to be an athlete.

But hang on just a moment,
There's one job I haven't thought,
It could be good or bad,
That job is only me!

Gina Aitken (9)

The World Is At Your Feet

The world is at your feet
Go on get off that lazy seat
Let it sweep you off your feet
And carry on to the land of dreams!
There you will find . . .
Your dream that you longed for
The world is at your feet!
Don't let your friends get you down
Or your smile will turn to a frown
The world is at your feet!

Jack Ramage (10)

I Want To Be A . . .

I want to be a punk rock star
And tour around the world,
I wouldn't be a teacher though
'Cause there's noisy boys and girls!

Office work sounds boring,
So does college maths,
But skateboarding with somebody cool,
Now that's my chosen path!

Or taking rides in my fancy car,
Maybe it'll be a Ferrari,
Or throwing darts at pictures of
The EastEnders guy called Barry!

Well here I am in primary,
Wishing my life away,
Reminding myself to never give up,
'Cause they could come true someday.

Jonathan Burns (10)

Living On A Desert Island

I live on this desert island,
Because it is like my own land,
My house is made out of sand
And one rubber band.

The island has lots of trees
And I do lots of wees,
Some people lose their knees,
All in the midsummer breeze.

All in one day
The children play,
But later today
We go to the bay.

Let's go to the sea,
That belongs to me,
Once I plea,
For the key (to find treasure island).

Jamie Freeman (8)

Happiness Is . . .

Happiness is a sweet sounding flute,
Keeping in tune by tapping my foot.

Happiness is red and gold,
The rich warm colours to keep out the cold.

Happiness is dancing in the rain,
Oh how exciting and there is no pain.

Happiness is a trip to Disney Land in France,
Oh how I would skip and dance.

Happiness is my granny,
I call her granny Annie.

Shauna Quinn (9)

If I Could . . .

If I could live in the sea
I'd join a fishy family
And I would swim all day long
Singing my fishy song

If I could live in the sea
I'd swim by the rocks and giggle with glee
And I'd make friends with an octopus
And we'd play hide and seek, so shush!

If I could go into space
I'd stare at an alien with a funny face
And I would visit the moon
And rap all day to an alien tune

If I could go into space
I'd go on a shooting star chase
And I'd float around 24/7
It would feel like being in Heaven

If I could be a tooth fairy
I could never, ever be scary
And I would take children's teeth
And give them to my handsome chief

If I could not go to school
My life would be really cool
I'd do something exciting every day
Then have a friend round for an overnight stay

If I could be in a comic
My power would be supersonic
I'd be a gymnast and a black belt
The hit of a bullet would feel like felt.

Rhiannon Heslop (9)

I Hope This Is Not A Dream

I hope this is not a dream
But I would love to play in a football team
To become as good as Giggs and Scholes
And score one of Van Nistlerooy's goals
To play along with the Neville brothers
Ronaldo, Keane, Butt and all the others
The live the life of a football star
And drive around in a big flashy car
I really want this dream to come true
To play in red and not in blue
And to play at The Old Trafford ground
Because Manchester United are the best team around.

Adam Derbyshire (9)

Horse Riding

H aving fun all the time
O ver the hills and far away
R iding and walking, trotting and jumping
S topping to drink at rivers and ponds
E ating from hedges at the side of the lane

R earing and bucking, ducking and snorting
I nside is good but outside is better
D ressage is easy, jumping is fun
I nto the wood then out in the sun
N earer and nearer you come to your stable
G allop for home while you are able.

The world at your feet!

Kirsty Hennen (9)

I Wish

I wish I could be a witch,
Zooming through the air.

I wish I could be a hairdresser,
Doing people's hair.

I wish I could be a shopkeeper,
Scanning people's food.

I wish I could be a mind-reader,
Checking people's mood.

I wish I could be an author,
Creating a story mixture.

I wish I could be an artist,
Painting a beautiful picture.

But whatever I choose to be,
I will always be me!

Carys Thomas (8)

My Hopes

M y hopes are to be a shopkeeper or an author
Y et maybe I'll be a teacher or maybe a spaceman

H oping I'll get lots of money
O n the TV I'll be or on the radio but people will see me every day
P eople will talk to me, chat to me and no one will laugh at me!
E very day when I wake, I will
S ee another hard day's work.

James Mitchell (10)

Hopes And Dreams

The world is at my feet,
Football is my life,
Football is me!

I've always wanted to be a footballer,
It has always been my dream,
But what if I'm not good enough?
What will I do instead?

If not football, the police will do,
I hope I could do the police patrol chases,
Or maybe a detective,
That's what I'll do!

Or maybe an actor
And be in Terminator 4, 5 or 6,
It would be fantastic,
To act on the TV.

I could be in the army,
I would have to work hard,
I could be in the army tank
And kill the enemy.

Well that's my hopes and dreams
And as I said,
The world is at my feet.

Paul Keiller (10)

Reach For The Stars

M y dream is to work for NASA
Y ou will see me on TV!

D uring the biggest ever space launch,
R ed planets, yellow planets and maybe an Earth,
E ven other humans or aliens
A nd I will return in 7 years,
M ega intelligent, with eight legs and 50 of my one-eyed friends,
   but now I'm sitting here in school, puzzling out 8x7!

Ross Currie (10)

Future

The world is at my feet,
I am going for gold!
I have to realise my dream!
Because dreams can come true!
The world is my oyster and now I have to choose,
What am I going to be?
What am I going to do?

Jamie Macdonald (10)

The Dream To Fantasy

My dream is to fly high above the sky,
To save people from dying,
To drive a Shelby Cobra, to see if anyone wants a ride,
To have magical powers,
So my fantasy will be to be a really good trained pilot.

Neil Kelly (9)

Hopes And Dreams

H eart beating dreams are magical things,
O nly you can say what your dream is,
P erhaps you want to work with animals, but
E veryone is different,
S ome people want to be rich

A nd I would like to be
N ormal,
D ancing is my biggest ambition.

D reams are magical things,
R unning through the world of
E xcitement,
A ll of them are sparkly and
M agical but I think mine might come true,
S o maybe they will! Someday . . .

Jenna Telfer (10)

Me And You

Don't let anybody nab your ambition,
I am going to be a rock star!
Screaming on the dance floor
And breaking down doors,
I love those kind of things,
That's mine!
What's yours?

Lisa Rarity (10)

Hopes And Dreams

D on't let anyone steal your hopes,
R unning for Scotland would be cool,
E veryone has hopes and dreams,
A mbulance driver would be good,
M aybe it will come true!
S ailing round the world would be amazing!

Sam Stuart (9)

Going For Gold

I've always wanted to be
The greatest footballer that ever lived.

I know I'm a girl but so what,
That could never stop me going for gold!

I want the skill of David Beckham,
I really want it so I'm going to get it!

I'm really going to practise hard
And let no one get in my way!

I really am going for gold,
I don't care what my mum says,
Because I'm going for gold!

I'm not very talented just yet,
But watch me, I'll do it,
I honestly will!

I'm going for gold,
No matter what you say,
Because I'm going for gold!

Alex Dickenson (10)

My Ambitions

M y ambition is fluttering about everywhere inside my head,
Y es I think I would love to be an art teacher

A nd study everything I can about art,
M y floating mind can't stop thinking about art,
B ooks of art make me so excited, I get all ticklish, I feel like I want to
   scream,
I love art so much, I wouldn't mind being a real experienced and expressive
   artist,
T oday, tomorrow, I'll never stop liking art all the same,
I think art is fantastic,
O h I think everyone should love art,
N o one is bad at art, everybody is even,
S o many people think that they are rubbish at art
   but everybody is the same, everybody is even!

Ellen Whillans (10)

My Dream!

Maybe I'll be rich one day,
Well, you never know.

Taking my mates for a ride in my fancy car,
Riding on my boogie board,
Down a giant hill,
Even better still, I may own a mansion.

Maybe I'll be rich one day,
Well, you never know!

Glen Muir (10)

What I Could Do . . .

I wonder what I could do if I could fly?
Could I fly to France? Maybe Spain?
Fly to Finland but if I fell, I would be in pain!
See Mount Everest or a volcano,
See George Bush and a tornado!
See the leaning Tower of Pisa,
Maybe stop for a pizza!
I do wonder what I could do if I could fly!

Fraser Stevenson (10)

Animals

A nimals are so, so cute,
N o other girl or boy can have my special dream,
I want to be the best animal lover,
M y future is to love and cuddle animals,
A nimals are so, so cute,
L onely they will never be because I love them all,
S o, so cute, so, so sweet and so, so soft.

Laia Greenan (10)

Going Bonkers On A BMX

When I'm older and I'm on my BMX,
I wonder if I could jump over a dinosaur or a T-Rex?
I would spin and swirl like a bird with one wing,
I would grind along the grinding post
And the pegs would go cling.
My downhill trial, black and a big scrape,
After a huge big crash or power-slide,
I would turn out like a grape!
I'd drop in a half-pipe trying hard not to fall,
But you've got to be careful you don't run into a wall,
I would wheelie and jump like a kangaroo,
I'd get so high I would need the loo,
BMXing is so much fun
But here I am at school sitting on my . . .
Seat!

Robbie Daly (10)

Untitled

When I grow up I would like to be a clown juggling sticks
Eat a Twix, jump a rope
And fall on a boat
Wear a coat, I'll ride a goat
I will wear pyjamas
While I slip on bananas
And slide on slippers.

Lauren Chapman (8)

My Life

I can't wait to leave school,
No more English and maths and French.
I'd like to go to a college or even a university.
I'd like to be an actress on stage and film
And maybe, marry Prince Charles!
That would be fun.

Jaillin Bates (9)

My Future Dream

There are many things to do in life,
It could be your dream come true.
I would perhaps want to look after animals
If they are sick or hurt badly,
My dream would be just that,
If only I had the chance to right now.
I would like to have lots of pets,
Just for myself,
That would be my life.

Amy Devitt (9)

Dreaming

There are many opportunities around us,
But not all are what we want.
Our dream may be . . .
Living in a mansion with a hundred rooms,
With a gigantic swimming pool
And many long winding slides leading into it
Or to be a pop star hitting number one on the top charts.
Maybe we just want to live a simple life,
With a family and many children.
Some may want to be a vet and work with puppies,
Kittens, hamsters, gerbils and many more.
But I want to be an author, writing many children's books
About castles, wizards, witches, dragons, unicorns and princesses,
Or anything else in a child's wide imagination.
My books will become films and I will be known by every child
In England and I'll be famous and wealthy and . . .
Well . . .
It is only a dream . . .
Isn't it?

Emily Wilkes (9)

My Dream

I dream of becoming an archaeologist
To go digging up dinosaurs,
Finding the skeletons of our old relatives
Or perhaps a Roman spear or two,
To then preserve them,
All the coins, bones and spears I'd found,
Or give them to a famous museum
And then travel the world to find a whole lot more!

Jessica Hawkes (9)

When I Grow Up

When I grow up I wish to go to Tonbridge Girls' Grammar School,
I would love to work at a restaurant as a waitress
Or I might be a scuba diver, jumping off the end of a cliff,
With the sunset beaming on it, like a daffodil,
I know I could be a horse riding teacher, now that would be fun,
But I might need to do an enormous amount of practise!
I think my best dream of all would to be a good athlete,
Like the amazing Paula Radcliff.

Cecilia Cole (9)

Fantasy World

The world at my feet, where should I go?
To the top of the mountain, the ocean below.

The world at my feet, where should I go?
To the top of my palace or the royal throne.

The world at my feet, where should I go?
Should I fly to the stars? Oh, I just don't know.

The world at my feet, where should I go?
Should I dance on the moon and watch the world glow?

The world at my feet, all my fantasies grow,
From one to another, until I get old.

Amarah St Aubyn (9)

I Wish I Had Super Powers

I wish I had super powers,
that lasted for hours.

I wish I could fly,
high in the sky.

I wish I could save people
that are caught high in the steeple.

I wish I could save my sister
because I really missed her.

I wish I could save the porter
who fell in the water.

I wish I could save the rat
which was being eaten by a cat.

I wish I could go back
to get on track.

Joseph Lalor (9)

A Whole New World!

All is peaceful, all is calm,
There is no war in sight,
No more hurting, no more harm,
All is soft and light.

The bluebirds singing sweetly
As they fly and sit on their branches,
A ballet dancer gracefully
Smiles and happily dances.

The sun and moon laugh together,
The clouds come greeting past,
Stars sparkle over the grounds,
While comets go shooting fast.

All people are friends,
No fighting can be seen,
You hear, 'Great!' when someone asks,
'Hello, how have you been?'

Amrita Pal (9)

Don't Be Afraid To Dream

Light, it gives you no fright
So don't be scared
The sun has risen
Light, it gives you no fright
Thank God it's day
No more dark for now
Don't be scared now the sun is up
Until the moon has raised
The sun is up
So wake up and don't be scared.

Kealan Gosney (10)

Colours

Colours are wonderful,
Colours are nice
Colours of the rainbow
Shine so bright
Colours mixed well, so beautiful
Colours are bright
Shining like my light
My favourite colour is pink
Which is the same colour as my sink
My jeans and my bedroom shine so bright
Like the colours of the rainbow in the night.

Janet Malomo (10)

Super Powers

Super powers, I can turn invisible
Super powers, I can be invincible
Super powers, I can easily trick a fool
Super powers, I'll never be a ghoul
Super powers, I can easily fly
Super powers, I will never die.

Super powers, to animals I can talk
Super powers, on water I can walk
Super powers, I am never wrong
Super powers, I am really strong
Super powers, I can see in the dark
Super powers, I can sing like a lark
Super powers, when I run I am the first,
Super powers, I never can be cursed.

Super powers, I would like to make them last
Super powers, but I know they will soon be past
Super powers, a childhood fantasy
Super powers, an ordinary adult I will be
Super powers, I am only seven
Super powers, they will be gone when I'm eleven.

Robert Potts (7)

The World At Our Feet

When I grow up, my future is . . .

I'd like to become a soap star,
To act in EastEnders,
To meet the crew!

I'd like to date Alfie Moon,
To meet Kat Slater
And Martin Fowler!

Maybe, just one day,
All my dreams will come true,
The next day I'll be rich!

I'll become famous,
So just one day I'll have . . .

The world at my feet!

Stephanie Weir (10)

Santa

Ho! Ho! Ho! It's me, Santa!
Have you been good or bad?
If you're bad, I'll be mad!
I have presents big and small,
You don't need to go to the mall.

Stefano Di Vito (9)

The Flower

I wish I was a flower
To enjoy the sun on my petals
The nettles beside me
And the grass near my leaves
It would be good to be a flower.

Jamie Bartle (8)

I Wonder

I wonder what it would be like if I
Could jump in a rocket and fly up high
Or if I could be a millionaire
And drive in a Ferrari without a care?

I wonder what it would be like if I
Could save the world or at least try
Or if I wrote a famous book?
People would give me a second look.

I wonder what it would be like if I
Could climb Mount Everest and touch the sky
Or if I could at least bring peace?
I'd truly have the world at my feet.

Mary Collins (11)

Golden Dream

Golden dream was running a stream
And saw lots of steam,
It could not bear people dying.

Golden dream was flying high,
Golden dream saw a pie,
Golden dream loved a fly,
Golden dream has never told a lie.

Golden dream walking on land
And then shook a hand,
Golden dream.

Harry Hughes (7)

If I Had Super Powers

If I had super powers,
I'd use them to do good
And if someone tried to stop me,
I'd turn them into a bee.

I'd also use my powers,
To do what I do best,
But if that doesn't satisfy me,
I'll be better than the rest.

This is one of my ambitions,
To be a witch or fairy,
But it wouldn't really be fair,
To be so nasty and scary.

Jessica Webb (10)

Appearing On Pop Idol

In Pop Idol you get a lot done
Dancing and singing, it is so much fun
And when you have done it
You have passed the test
For singing at my very best

People getting to the top
For boogying to the hippy hop
All the girls singing away
When the boys sing, 'Hip hip hooray!'

Nevertheless I will not get through
For singing and dancing all day for you
But I will have a little go
And if I don't get through then, oh no!

Lucy Till (9)

Having Super Powers

If I had super powers
I'd zap him right now!
If I had super powers
I could fly high in the sky

It would be great to have super powers
I could do anything I like
I could have my favourite toy
Whenever I like

If I had super powers
I'd clean my bedroom in a zoom
If I had super powers
I'd fly to the moon and back

That's what I'd do
If I had super powers!

Emily Harris (8)

Having Super Powers

S uper powers are the best,
U sing them can be a pest,
P oking power is really good,
E very power can save towns,
R eally useful when you're down.

P owers can really help you,
O ver the road cannot cross, I'll be there for you,
W ow! Zapping people as you go,
E very day you're never slow,
R eady, steady, off we goooooo!
S o once again the day is saved by the super powers!

Jodie Lydall (8)

If I Had Super Powers

If I had super powers
I'd give him a pow
Not today but
Right now!

If I had super powers
I'd be a right kick
I'd be very rich
So I'll make my pick!

If I had super powers
I'd be super strong
I'd be good at cleaning my bedroom
But not the pong!

Now I'm very tired
Right in my head
I'm going somewhere
And that's my bed!

Joe Sharp (8)

Fighting Evil

F ighting evil would be an easy thing
I would fight a lot of people and always win
G oing to war would be scary
H aving to go and fight would be scary
T o fight evil is my dream
I would go down as the best fighter in the world
N ever would I stay at home
G oing to fight is me

E very time I go to fight, I am full of fright
V ery scared
I n a secret place
L ost in a lonely world.

Jack Randall (9)

When I Grow Up I Want To Be . . .

A builder who drives trucks
An aeroplane pilot
Be an artist
Be a millionaire
Own a mansion
Be a racer.

Danny Grayson (7)

When I Grow Up I Want To Be . . .

To rule the world so I can have a pool
A swimmer to swim from Hull to India
A manager for the Spanish team Real Madrid
A king of the world
A professional player for Real Madrid
A person that is real funny.

Liam Hopkins (7)

When I Grow Up I Want To Be . . .

A pop star so everyone can look at me at home
A shopkeeper
A hairdresser
A park keeper
A pencil sharpener.

Naomi McLaren (7)

When I Grow Up I Want To Be . . .

The Queen and have lots of money
And have a pet giraffe
I wish I was a princes
And be called Matilda
I want to be an artist
And draw lots of pictures.

Leonie Tovey-Hales (7)

When I Grow Up I Want To Be . . .

A hairdresser that does people's hair
A pop star on TV
Someone who flies a plane
Someone who works as a gymnast
A millionaire in a fancy house.

Jade Hall (7)

When I Grow Up I Want To Be . . .

A Scottish dancer who wears a kilt
A pop idol who sings on TV
I want to be a teacher who helps people
I want to be a vet who helps dogs and cats
I want to be an aeroplane pilot who helps people
Someone who owns a pool with a slide.

Fiona Hodgson (7)

When I Grow Up I Want To Be . . .

A wrestler who wrestles a crocodile
An Egyptian who dances in a pyramid
A fireman that fights fire.

Nathan Bunting (7)

When I Grow Up I Want To Be . . .

A pop star on TV
I want to be a princess and live for a million years
I want to be a nurse and help people when they're poorly
Be on a girls football team and score lots of goals
I want to be on CBBC and tell lots of jokes.

Rebecca Casey (7)

When I Grow Up I Want To Be . . .

A pop idol who sings on TV
When I grow up I want to be
A scanner which scans food
When I grow up I want to be
A gymnastic lady.

Demi-Leigh Mills (7)

Super Powers

S uper powers are so great
U sing them is not a pest
P eople think the mud pie trick is best
E veryone knows me really well
R rrr! Goes the Devil down in Hell

P eople scream and here I come
O w! And the Devil's dead
W ell I do have a bruise on my head
E very day a crime goes on
R eally bad sometimes
S uper powers are so great.

Ellie Taylor (8)

Living On A Desert Island

D eserts are hot, deserts are cool
E ven though there's no swimming pool
S et sail to the desert pond
E veryone has a play
R egular fish swim away
T hink of fish down below

I sland far away here we come
S harks are here, even if there are no fish
L ove the desert even though
A shark is there, watch out below
N o place is better than a desert
D eserts are hot and deserts are cool.

Daniel Russell (8)

Driving A Ferrari

F erraris racing round a track
E ach car is really fast
R acing in the pits
R acing on a track
A Ferrari can win every race
R acing round the German track
I lead the race, no doubt about that!

Daniel Wildman (8)

Having Super Powers

H aving the world on my own
A nd I can kill easy as gold
V olvo is my name
I have special powers
N o more evil monsters
G oing round the world

S un to moon
U p in the sky
P ieces of silver
E vil to good
R olling in a steamroller.

P owers of bronze
O n the horizon
W et and dry
E asy and hard
R olling in a bulldozer
S uperhero, that's me!

Cameron Nash (8)

Ferrari

F riday I had a lovely day
E very day me and my friend go to the park
R oughly we'd play
R eally we heard a dog bark
A nd it was May
R eally it was dark
I say it is the end of the day.

Joe Haycock (8)

What I Would Like To Be

When I grow up I'd like to be a clown
And wear pyjamas while slipping on bananas
There will be bears
And I'd make them pears
The cats will live under the mats.

Katie Johnston (8)

Being In A Football Team

F ootball is my destiny
O ut on the field as good as I could be
O n the way as fast as a cheetah
T he ball is mine and I will battle on for it
B eing the best is my goal
A ll the players will cheer for me
L augh and giggle if you want, we will beat you 3-1
L eft on the field, crying and sulking, covered in mud
    dreaming of the golden cup.

Lamar Harrison (9)

Chemist

C uring people
H ealing wounds
E lement study
M aking potions
I always know
S cientific explorations
T hat's the right job for me.

Wilfie Diskin (9)

When I'm Older

When I'm older I'm going to be rich,
When I'm older I'm going to live next to a football pitch,
When I'm older I'm going to be a star,
When I'm older I'm going to drive a car,
When I'm older I'm going to have three girls,
When I'm older I'm going to have curls,
When I'm older I'm going to be married,
When I'm older I'm going to have a horse and carriage,
When I'm older I'm going to buy a mansion,
When I'm older my kids won't have a tantrum,
When I'm older I'm going to be happy,
When I'm older I'm going to change my children's nappy.

Jade Monks (9)

Journey To Mars

I'm going to the future
I told my mum and dad one day
They looked up from the TV screen
But they had nothing to say
I went to ask my brother
But he was only four
So after the reply, 'Waa waa'
I backed out through the door
I packed my little suitcase
With loads of choccy bars
'That should keep me going'
On my journey towards Mars
And when I finally get there
I will show them life on Mars
A photo of me eating
My lovely chocolate bars.

Adam Davis (10)